# FEAR NOT

# ALSO BY SAM POLSON

*In His Image*
(English, Romanian, Mandarin, & Spanish)

*By Faith*
(English & Romanian)

*SonLight:*
*Daily Light from the Pages of God's Word*

*Corona Victus: Conquering the Virus of Fear*
(English & Romanian)

*Life Changing Prayer*

*The Climbing Angel Christmas Treasury*
(An anthology containing multiple authors)

*Pathways:*
*Ancient Paths from the Pages of the Old Testament*

*My Mother's Bible*
(part of the Single Sermon Series)

# FEAR NOT

### God's Peace For Navigating
### the Storms of Life

SAM POLSON

Publishing
Angel
Climbing

FEAR NOT
Written by Sam Polson

R.E.A.P. Guides by Joe Kappel
Edited by Lisa Soland

Text copyright © 2024 Sam Polson

Published in 2024 by:
Climbing Angel Publishing
PO Box 32381
Knoxville, Tennessee 37930
http://www.ClimbingAngel.com

First Edition: November 2024
     (Revised from *Corona Victus,* published in 2020)
Printed in the United States of America
Author photo by Stefan Holt
Graphic design by Climbing Angel Publishing

ISBN: 978-1-956218-41-1
Library of Congress Control Number: 2024921566

This book is lovingly dedicated
to my sister-in-law, Carol Bittner,
who won her Victor's Crown
April 6, 2020

# CONTENTS

# FOREWORD

F ear has a long history with the human race. After Adam and Eve sinned in the garden, they tried to hide themselves from the presence of the Lord. When the Lord called for Adam, saying, "Where are you?" Adam answered, "I heard the sound of you in the garden, and I was afraid, because I was naked, and I hid myself" (Gen. 3:10). When sin entered God's perfect creation, there were consequences. Fear was one of those consequences, and we have been dealing with it ever since. The problem of fear itself was bad enough, but Adam compounded his difficulties by trying to solve it his own way, apart from God. He hid himself from the Lord, or so he thought. Of course, his Heavenly Father knew exactly what he had done and where he was all the time.

If we are truthful with ourselves, we must admit that things haven't changed much since then. We still sin, and we still struggle with fear. We also struggle with how to deal with fear, often doing the exact opposite of what we should do, just like Adam! More often than not, we try to resolve our fear apart from the One who loves and understands us like no other.

Today, we live in a world gripped with fear in many ways. Just a few years ago, we experienced a global pandemic that almost paralyzed the world economy, isolating millions of people and still affecting the way many of us live our lives. The tragic reality of war is something multitudes are dealing with now, and the potential threat of those wars growing and impacting our nation can be a very frightening proposition. Political unrest, climate issues, and economic concerns are all around us and help to foster an environment of fear. There seems to be a never-ending list of things that can strike fear in our hearts today. We desperately need Biblical answers to combat this problem, which has plagued humanity throughout history and is as strong an adversary today as ever. We must find a way to move toward our Savior instead of away from Him.

In *Fear Not*, Pastor Sam Polson takes us on a journey through the Scriptures to help us combat the foe of fear we all encounter at times. I have known Sam for over 30 years. For the last 20, he has been my pastor, and since 2019, I have had the privilege of serving on staff under his leadership at West Park Baptist Church in Knoxville, Tennessee. I count him as a dear friend and mentor. His practical wisdom and shepherd's heart have been such a blessing to me in my walk with Jesus. I have worked alongside him as we navigated the fearful difficulties of the COVID-19 pandemic and other ministry challenges every church experiences. I have witnessed his unwavering trust in Jesus and his commitment to walk out Biblical truth repeatedly. Pastor Sam has an extraordinary way of clarifying God's truth and helping others apply it to the everyday situations we find ourselves in. His wisdom is not just theoretical but practical, giving us the tools we need to face our fears head-on.

This book is more than a list of theological truths to help us deal with fear. It is the work of a seasoned pastor who knows how to point God's people to the One who loves us and gave Himself for us. Knowing and following Jesus truly is the antidote to fear and every other problem of the human heart. I know you will be blessed with this book as Pastor Sam uses God's word to help transform our fears into faith and our despairs into hope in Jesus, who helps us *Fear Not*!

James Alan Lynch
*Senior Adult Director & Minister of Pastoral Care*
*Knoxville, TN*

# INTRODUCTION

I n early 2020, I was traveling to a mission board meeting in another state when all the federal guidelines for implementing "social distancing" were first announced to the nation. Our elders and staff immediately made plans via "social networking" to prepare for the coming Sunday gathering without actually being able to gather. I certainly found it incredibly strange when Sunday arrived to be sitting at a desk in a hotel room watching the first live stream broadcast of a worship service taking place in the church that I pastor. All of it was going on without me being there! But I was also blessed to experience, along with my congregation, true *spiritual connecting* even as we gathered by means of the internet in a season of "*social distancing*." I was deeply encouraged to sense that what binds us together as God's people crosses all boundaries of location or isolation.

So often, our Lord uses the challenging experiences in our lives to provide deeper experiences with him. It is my sincere hope that this book will be used by our Heavenly Father to bring peace to your soul when it seems as if every landmark in your life is being shaken or even obliterated. It is only natural that in such seasons, we experience the very natural emotion of fear. However, there exists a power that can be felt in the deepest regions of our soul that is much more powerful and much more real than fear, and that is God's peace. His is a peace that truly surpasses all understanding and guards our hearts and minds by the power of Jesus Christ himself (Phil. 4:7). Fear is powerful, but it is not ALL powerful. The power that reigns supreme over all is the power of the One who is the

Master of seas. My prayer as you read the following pages is to hear deeply in your spirit His strong voice saying, "Fear Not."

Sam Polson
*October 2024*
*Knoxville, TN*

# HOW TO R.E.A.P.
## THE WORD OF GOD

**R**ead: Read the passage carefully and prayerfully.

**E**xamine: Read the passage again, noting keywords or phrases. Be careful to note the context surrounding the passage. Ask questions about the passage. Who is the audience? What situation is the speaker or author addressing? What is the main theme of this passage? Note, in particular, what you learn about the Lord from the passage.

**A**pply: Consider carefully the impressions on your heart as you read. How does this passage touch on specific areas or situations in your life? What wisdom are you gaining from this passage? What are you learning about your Lord in relation to your current spiritual experience?

**P**ray: Use what the Lord has revealed about himself or you personally as an opportunity to respond directly to him. Pray to him in praise, repentance, or petition for others as the Holy Spirit guides you. Treat this time in God's Word not as a devotional exercise but as a personal encounter with your Holy God and your loving Savior.

# - 1 -

# THE PRINCE AT PEACE

*On that day, when evening had come, he said to
them, "Let us go across to the other side." And
leaving the crowd, they took him with them in the
boat, just as he was. And other boats were with him.
And a great windstorm arose, and the waves were
breaking into the boat, so that the boat was already
filling. But he was in the stern, asleep on the
cushion. And they woke him and said to him,
"Teacher, do you not care that we are perishing?"
And he awoke and rebuked the wind and said to the
sea, "Peace! Be still!" And the wind ceased, and there
was a great calm. He said to them, "Why are you so
afraid? Have you still no faith?" And they were filled
with great fear and said to one another, "Who then
is this, that even the wind and the sea obey him?"*
(Mark 4:35-41)

B efore January 2020, I am sure very few of us had ever heard of the word coronavirus. Now, we know the word all too well, whether by personal experience or by its impact on our family or friends. Most definitely, we are all aware that this virus changed our world. Perhaps the way the coronavirus most changed our culture is the deeper and even more deadly spiritual and emotional virus that it fueled. I am talking about the virus of fear. Vince Lombardi, a famous football coach, said, "Fear makes cowards of us all." However, in the lives of believers, fear can do something much worse than make us cowards. Fear makes us forget *who* we are, forget *whose* we are, and forget the meaning and mission of our lives on this planet. Fear is a virus that is deadly not only to our lives but to our minds and our very souls.

I remember feeling the effects of that fear in the early days of the coronavirus outbreak. I attended a mission board meeting in Pennsylvania. On the opening morning of the sessions, I realized I had forgotten something in my car and headed to the parking lot to retrieve it. As I was going down the back stairs, I met a friend coming up. Harry is a missionary physician and a wonderful and talented follower of the Lord. We warmly greeted each other, and then, of course, our conversation quickly landed on how we were dealing with the impact of the coronavirus pandemic.

Harry said, "Hey, let me read to you an email someone just sent me. It's a quote in a letter from Martin Luther as Germany, in the 16th century, was visited by an outbreak of the bubonic plague." My friend continued to explain that Martin Luther was asked how he would respond to the virus, and here is what Luther wrote back to his friend.

> *"I shall ask God mercifully to protect us. Then I shall fumigate, help purify the air, administer medicine, and take it. I shall avoid places and persons where my presence is not needed in order not to become*

*contaminated and thus perchance infect and pollute others, and so cause their death as a result of my negligence. If God should wish to take me, he will surely find me and I have done what he has expected of me and so I am not responsible for either my own death or the death of others. If my neighbor needs me, however, I shall not avoid place or person but will go freely, as stated above. See, this is such a God-fearing faith because it is neither brash nor foolhardy and does not tempt God."*
(Martin Luther, *Luther's Works*, Vol. 43: *Devotional Writings II*, ed. Jaroslav Jan Pelikan, Hilton C. Oswald, and Helmut T. Lehmann, vol. 43 (Philadelphia: Fortress Press, 1999), 119–38.

What a great statement with such powerful encouragement. Although that answer from the great reformer was written 500 years ago, it is timeless and timely in its application to any season of fear that, like a raging storm, sweeps into our lives. Fear is so powerful, but it is not *all-powerful*. That quality belongs only to the One who is the originator and completer of our faith. Fear-conquering faith comes from keeping Jesus as the focus of our faith.

In Mark 4:35-41, we have a recorded storm story, not from the Weather Channel but from the Word of God. This story from the life of Jesus teaches us how to keep our bearings by keeping a faith focus during the storms of life. In this passage of Scripture, we find four truths on which to focus during our stormy times.

## 1. THE PROVIDENCE OF GOD

The word providence means "control" or "guidance." The doctrine of God's providence undergirds everything we believe. All of life itself is supported by this truth of God's sovereign providence. Divine providence means that this universe is not governed by randomness. The universe in which we live and have our being is guided by rationality and intentionality that comes from God himself. In general application, Divine providence means that God, our Lord, permits all that happens. That is true, but we need to be careful. God *is not* the author of sin. "God is light, and in him is no darkness at all" (1 John 1:5).

God is not the author of sin, so he is not the author of its consequences, which is the curse of sin on the world in which we live. The curse of sin is in all of us as fallen image-bearers. God is not the author of sin, yet God, in his divine providence, permits sin and its consequences to continue for a season. It is difficult to fully comprehend that providence means our Lord God permits all that happens.

I vividly remember Sunday, September 16, 2001. The churches were not empty; they were overflowing because of a national crisis that took place on Tuesday, September 11, or as we know it, 9/11. I recall being contacted by a local television station that weekend and asked if I would do a live interview Sunday at 6:30 a.m. When the segment began on live television, the first question the reporter asked me was, "So, Reverend Polson, why did God allow this to happen?"

My first thought was, "Six-thirty in the morning, and you're asking me that kind of question?!" But inside my mind, I quickly prayed and then provided the reporter with the answer. (And I believe it was a biblical answer.) I said simply, "I don't know. And neither does anyone else." The truth is we don't know the answer to some things. The answers reside in the realm of Divine providence, and only God knows.

One of the most important verses in the Word of God on this subject, which I believe will undergird your life and faith, is Deuteronomy 29:29:

> *The secret things belong to the Lord our God, but the*
> *things that are revealed belong to us and to our*

*children forever, that we may do all the words of this law.*

Now, notice in that verse this phrase: "The secret things belong to the Lord our God..." We do not know his plans for the things that he has not revealed. We cannot understand his mind. We don't know those things, but the things he has revealed are ours to receive, believe, and pass on to our children. Divine providence does not mean that life is a cosmic chess game with people as the pawns on God's chessboard. There is a gracious application of God's divine providence at work, which means our Lord has a plan for all things that happen to his people, and it is a gracious plan.

This story in Mark, Chapter 4, perfectly illustrates Divine providence. The storm rocked all the boats out in the sea that day, but the Lord had a specific plan for his followers who were in one particular boat. It is very important to recognize that the disciples were not in this boat and this storm because they were *out of the will of God*. They were in this boat and this storm because they were *in the will of God*. The Lord Jesus Christ himself led his disciples into this boat and allowed them to sail into this storm. Their journey that day was a gracious plan of the Lord, who loved them.

Now, when this storm swept over the disciples, Romans 8:28 had not yet been written with the inspired quill of the Apostle Paul. But what Paul wrote at a later date communicated an eternal truth:

*And we know that for those who love God all things work together for good, for those who are called according to his purpose.*
(Romans 8:28)

Consider that verse. I mean, really, look at that verse. Do you believe, *really* believe, that this statement is true?

Regardless of the storms and their physical and emotional distress, the promise of God is still true. "And we know that for those who love God all things work together for good, for those who are called according to his purpose." Perhaps, my friend, where you are right now, you need to get really honest with Jesus by saying, "Lord, I believe; help my unbelief!" (Mark 9:24). It is the honest cry of a struggling heart. *"I don't understand this; I can't wrap my mind around it because 'the secret things' belong to you, Lord. But this promise of Romans 8:28 has been revealed by you, and it is for me. I know this. Now, Lord God, please help me to take hold of this and believe it. Help me to believe in you during the storms of life, even this storm occurring in my life right now."*

## 2. PEACE OF OUR LORD

We can shelter through any storm in the providence of our Lord Jesus Christ. But *how* do we do that? How do we shelter ourselves in the providence of our gracious Lord? By focusing on something else. We focus on *someone* else. We focus on the peace of our Lord!

Let's look at the two incredible contrasts going on in this boat. On the one hand, you have the disciples who are struggling, yelling, and bailing out water for all they're worth. And now let's look at Jesus—sweetly napping in the stern of the boat without a wrinkle on his brow. He is surely the *Prince at peace.*

These disciples are made of the same human stuff we are made of now, and they are filled with fear. Jesus is in a quiet peace in the midst of their storm. He is resting peacefully, and this incredibly frustrates the disciples. Their fear becomes frustration with their Lord, who seems to be resting so comfortably while they are at such risk. That is why we are told in Mark 4:38 that they exclaimed, "Teacher, do you not care that we are perishing?" *How can you sleep so serenely while we are about to die here?!*

6

That question has been asked untold billions of times over the centuries. "Lord, do you not care that we are perishing?!" I wonder how many times in the last few years that cry has gone up from the people of God? There is a reality communicated here that we need to be honest about. Storms can cause us to *forget*. Storms can cause us to forget important things very quickly. We have this very human tendency, which is part of our fallenness, to forget in the storms what we learned in the calm. We tend to forget in the darkness what we learned in the light.

> We forget in the darkness what
> we learned in the light.

What is it that these disciples have forgotten? They have forgotten *who is onboard the boat*. They have forgotten *who is in the boat with them*. And in the providence of God, they are about to be reminded. This is God's *gracious* providence. This storm is a gracious gift to them, as they will be reminded of an incredible truth they will never forget for the rest of their lives. They are going to be reminded of the *power of the Lord*.

### 3. THE POWER OF THE LORD

Mark 4:39 tells us, "And he awoke and rebuked the wind and said to the sea, 'Peace! Be still!' And the wind ceased, and there was a great calm." The fearful storm that threatened to flood and sink the boat was subdued by the words of Jesus. This display of power caused another flood, a flood of fear that entered the hearts of these disciples. It was a different kind of fear than the fear of the storm. The awe-filled fear was expressed this way in verse 41, "Who then is this, that even the wind and the sea obey him?" They were speechless. "*Who can this be that is in this boat with us that the very wind and sea must obey?*" The disciples were speechless, but Jesus was not.

It was now his turn to speak and their turn to listen. It was his turn to ask them a very probing question.

In Mark 4:40, Jesus asked them, "Why are you so afraid? Have you still no faith?" The One who had just rebuked the wind and the waves now rebukes their weakness—the weakness of their faith. You see, fear made them faithless. They had allowed their fear to lead them to faithlessness. How did that happen? How did fear take away their faith? It took their faith away because their focus shifted. Fear had changed their focus. In their fear, their focus became fixated *on the disaster* that was threatening them rather than *the master* who was with them.

> In their fear, they forgot who was with them.

I want to tell you, shipmates, fear makes us forget who is on board in our lives. The old gospel song "Master, the Tempest Is Raging," written by Mary Ann Baker, shares our struggle:

> *Master, the tempest is raging*
> *Oh, The billows are tossing high*
> *The sky is o'ershadowed with blackness*
> *Oh, No shelter or help is nigh*
> *Carest thou not that we perish?*
> *How canst thou lie asleep*
> *When each moment so madly is threatning*
> *A grave in the angry deep?*

Fear makes us forget the truth. And what is the truth? It is the same truth that this gospel song by Mary Ann Baker shares:

8

*Whether the wrath of the storm-tossed sea*
*Or demons or men or whatever it be,*
*No waters can swallow the ship where lies*
*The Master of ocean and earth and skies.*

That is the truth, and we cannot let ourselves forget it in the midst of fear.

Jesus' challenge to his disciples about their fear was a challenge to faith. Where was their object of faith? Their object of faith rested in Jesus. It was not faith in their faith. It was certainly not faith in their circumstances. But their faith that he challenged was their faith in him. In effect, what Jesus is challenging them to remember is to *remember him.* My friend, that is how we stay in faith and keep walking in faith. That is how we overcome fear—when our focus remains on him, the Master of ocean and earth and sky. The Master is in the boat. Our Master is in *our* boat. He is our Prince, and he is at peace. He is in the boat with us.

What is Jesus saying through this timely story? He is saying to his followers throughout the ages, to us as his people in this very fearful time in which we live right now, "Remember me in this storm. Focus on me in this storm, and you will have faith."

### 4. THE PRESENCE OF THE LORD

This is our challenge today—to remember the presence of the Lord. And that is the fourth focus of these gospel verses. The Lord never promised that we would not go through storms. In fact, the truth is just the opposite. Jesus said, "In the world you will have tribulation. But take heart; I have overcome the world" (John 16:33). Jesus did not promise that we would not go through storms. What he did promise was that we would never go through a single storm alone.

He promised, "And behold, I am with you always, to the end of the age" (Matt. 28:20). Jesus shared this just before he

9

ascended into Heaven. *"No matter what comes, don't forget—I am with you always. Always!"*

Dear friend, a Christian can be many things, but one thing he or she can never be is *alone*. Never. Ever. Today, the Lord is in your boat because he is in your heart if you are a Christian. He is in you. Christ in you is the hope of glory. So, in any circumstance or situation that you are in, whatever it may be—you are not alone because Jesus is not just with you; he is *within you*. The Lord Jesus Christ himself, by his Spirit, is in your heart right now.

I want to challenge you to declare this at this very moment. Just say it out loud. *"He is with me."* Or better still, if you are gathered as a family or as a couple, sharing this book together in Bible study right now, simply declare this together, *"He is with us."* If you don't know that Christ is in you, then know this—the fiercest storm in life is nothing compared to the storm of the wrath of God that awaits those who reject his Son, the Lord Jesus.

If you don't have that peace in your heart today, if you don't know that the Master of ocean and earth and sky is in your heart, that he is your very life, and he lives within you, then I beg you right now, wherever you are, kneel before the Maker of Heaven and Earth, the Lord Jesus Christ. Call upon him in faith and ask him to forgive your sins. Trust him as your Lord and Savior. Surrender your life to him, and he will speak his peace into your heart—the peace that surpasses all understanding—the peace of his salvation. He will say to you, "Peace, be still."

I pray that through this time of providence, you will be led to see that there is only one unchanging certainty and absolute safety, and that is in Jesus Christ our Lord. To know him and to have him as your Savior is to know peace. I pray that this will be your experience this very hour. And that God will confirm this truth in your heart through his Spirit. I pray that the Lord speak into your storm right now, just as he spoke into the storm with his disciples that day, "Peace, be still."

# PRAYER

*Almighty God and Heavenly Father, we thank you for being an infinite God. You are infinite in your glory, majesty, and mercy, for you are merciful to all who call upon you. You are full of kindness and compassion. Lord God, we pray that you will make us vessels of that compassion in ministry as we have the opportunity. We thank you for your peace. We pray that your peace will reign right now in our hearts and lives. We pray that your peace will come to those who trust in you and surrender to you as Lord and Savior. O, Lord God, we pray you will grant mercy to our country and this world. Grant us your grace so that we may faithfully serve you by serving others in their times of fear and struggle. May we be instruments of your peace, Lord Jesus. We pray that you will keep our eyes focused on you and remind us that you are not far away but with us in every circumstance. We are not alone. We praise you for this and give you glory.*

*Amen.*

# R.E.A.P. GUIDE

**R**EAD

- Read Mark 4:35-41.
- What do you think the Holy Spirit intends to teach us from this passage?

**E**XAMINE

- What is the time of day when this account happens (35)?
- The storm that came on Jesus and the disciples was sudden; there was no way the disciples could have planned around it. How is the storm described? How did the disciples react during the storm?
- When they woke Jesus, what did he immediately do? What happened to the storm?
- Jesus rebuked the disciples for what reason?
- In the end, the disciples no longer fear the storm. What do they fear now, and why?

**A**PPLY

- In what ways have you been tempted to fear during a challenging season?
- During times of fear, how do you identify with the disciples who doubted the Lord's care for them?
- What have you learned about the Lord Jesus from this account that will help you conquer fear?

**P**RAY

- Using the "PRAY" acronym, respond with **P**raise to the Lord, **R**epent of sins this Bible passage has revealed to you, **A**sk the Lord for any requests you have, and **Y**ield to his will.

# - 2 -

# THE FOCUS OF FAITH

*Therefore, since we are surrounded by so great a
cloud of witnesses, let us also lay aside every
weight, and sin which clings so closely, and let us
run with endurance the race that is set before us,
looking to Jesus, the founder and perfecter of our
faith, who for the joy that was set before him
endured the cross, despising the shame, and is
seated at the right hand of the throne of God.*
(Hebrews 12:1-2)

I shared in the introduction what an unusual experience it
was for me to be out of town and watch the first live-
streaming worship service at my own church that first Sunday
after the establishment of the national "social distancing"
guidelines. It occurred to me then that no one was actually
sitting in the auditorium. All the congregants were watching
the service online, just like me. That was different, for sure.

But that unusual moment was far surpassed the following Sunday when the most *surreal moment* I have ever had in ministry occurred.

On that beautiful morning, I pulled into the West Park Baptist parking lot at about 9:25, and there before me was a grand total of four vehicles. Usually, at that time, there would be hundreds of cars parked there. I then entered the auditorium and found it *empty;* only a handful of people were there, preparing to lead the online worship service. An empty auditorium on Sunday morning! A pastor's nightmare! Eventually, two other men sat with me, using appropriate "social distancing," and as our worship pastor and small praise team led in songs of worship, the three of us joined in with all of our hearts. Our voices created quite a unique blend. I'm sure there is no auditorium anywhere that we cannot empty! Delivering the sermon, I gave it my very best to share the message in a personal and engaging way, although I was speaking to an empty auditorium. I spoke into a camera *I could not see* and to an audience *that was not visible.* Other than that, it was a pretty typical preaching experience.

But it was actually *following* the service when I experienced the *most surreal moment* in my entire ministry. At about 11:45, I walked through the buildings on the campus of our church on a Sunday morning, and they were completely empty. Usually, there would be crowds in every hallway—children and adults running about—but now, all the space was completely empty. I walked through the welcome center—empty. I came back into the auditorium—empty. But most of all, my heart was empty. And that is when it happened. The Spirit of the Lord clearly spoke to my heart. I deeply sensed him saying to me, *"See this, Sam. See this!"* And here is what I saw. In an *empty church building*, I saw *the church body.* It was perhaps the greatest reminder of my life that the church is not brick-and-mortar or a building. The actual church is a body, the body of Christ, and that morning, *we had gathered* as that body just as sure as if we had met together physically.

But more than that, millions of our brothers and sisters in Christ all over the world gathered together that Sunday, even though their buildings were also empty. That was a great moment for me. I understood that the body of Christ *was* together, gathering in Spirit and in Truth. God so encouraged me by allowing me to *see the invisible.*

Sometimes, the Lord Jesus Christ transforms our trials into our greatest triumphs. Certainly, we all experience intense times of trial, but through our Lord, these can become times of triumph.

In the previous chapter, we discussed the Lord's providence. We learned that God, in his providence, allows us to experience trials so that we can learn to *view the invisible* and *value the invaluable.* It is in times of trial that the Lord helps us to truly *see* the invisible so we can more *value* what is *invaluable.*

We considered this truth in Chapter 1 as we read the story recorded in the Gospel of Mark, Chapter 4, of the disciples in the boat during a terrible storm. The boat was about to sink, but Jesus was sound asleep, taking a nap in the stern of the boat. In a frantic state, the disciples woke him, asking, "Master, don't you care that we are perishing?" Jesus stood and rebuked the wind and the waves, and a calm came over the sea. Then, the awe-struck disciples asked themselves, "Who is this that even the winds and the seas obey him?" Do you remember the question Jesus asked them? He asked, "Why are you so afraid? Do you still have no faith?" Notice that Jesus connected the *fullness of fear* with a *failure of faith.* The fullness of fear that had controlled his disciples was really the result of a *failure of faith.* What did Jesus want his disciples to see in this storm?

### Jesus wanted the disciples to see *him.*

Jesus was asleep in their boat. He was their Prince at peace. And if the Prince is at peace, his people do not have to be overcome with fear. Friends, Jesus is always in our boat. He was the disciples' peace over 2000 years ago, and he is our peace today. It is in seeing him that our faith is created, and it is in seeing Jesus that our faith is also sustained. The keyword is "seeing."

> Faith must have a focus.

If we look *within ourselves*, we will not find much cause for faith. If we focus on what is going on around us, we won't find much there to bring faith either. But if we fix our eyes on Jesus, that is where faith is both created and sustained. Let's reflect on the passage that communicates this truth so beautifully—Hebrews 11. Notice what the writer of Hebrews reveals to us about faith.

### WHAT IS FAITH?

The Book of Hebrews is a challenge for professing believers in the Messiah. In reading this scripture, we are challenged to persevere through difficult times by the power of faith. The author is speaking to believers who were going through terrible times of trial. The challenge is, "Don't turn back to unbelief; press on in faith." So we must ask the question again, "What is faith?" In Hebrews, Chapter 11, verses 1-2, the author shares with us the essence of faith:

> *Now faith is the assurance of things hoped for, the*
> *conviction of things not seen. For by it the people of*
> *old received their commendation.*

The writer of Hebrews gives us some wonderful examples to ensure we truly understand faith. Beginning in verses 7 through 40, we are provided examples of famous, infamous, and even unknown followers of God through the centuries. They are radically different in character and experience, yet they are all united by the one common denominator of faith.

We must remember that the original text of Scripture did not have chapter divisions, so even though we move from Chapter 11 to Chapter 12, the theme of the writer's thoughts regarding faith continues. He defines the *essence* of faith and then describes several *examples* of faith. As Chapter 12 begins, the author shares with us what faith looks like and how it is expressed.

### WHAT DOES FAITH LOOK LIKE?

If we are supposed to be people of faith, what does this expression of faith look like? There is a simple but profound answer, so please don't miss this—faith looks a lot like "looking."

One of the greatest quotes on faith that I have ever read is from the pastor and author A. W. Tozer, who served many years ago in Chicago, Illinois. This quote has sustained me through many hardships. A. W. Tozer said, "Faith is the gaze of the soul upon a saving God."

**"Faith is the gaze of a soul upon a saving God."
(A.W. Tozer)**

Throughout the Bible, we see "looking" connected with believing and having faith. Faith is the gaze of the soul. Where and how does faith gaze on the Lord? Faith gazes upon the Lord, our saving God, *through prayer*.

One of the greatest times of trial for the nation of Judah took place under the time of their good king, Jehoshaphat. Judah was attacked by a terrible enemy—the amassed armies of the Moabites and the Ammonites. Their attack was going to be horrific, possibly producing a 100% mortality rate. The people felt powerless. "What can we do against such an enemy?" They were consumed with fear. We understand that, don't we? They felt so powerless against this invading enemy. Then, even though he was afraid, King Jehoshaphat *acted*. He called the people into fasting and prayer. Jehoshaphat himself led them in prayer, and it is one of the most beautiful prayers in the Bible. I want us to focus on one phrase from this prayer. It appears in 2 Chronicles 20:12. Here is what the King of Judah prayed to God:

> *"O our God, will you not execute judgment on them?*
> *For we are powerless against this great horde that*
> *is coming against us. We do not know what to do,*
> *but our eyes are on you."*

"We do not know what to do, but our eyes are on you." Isn't that beautiful? They were looking to God in prayer. Their eyes were on him as they were praying. The people of God kept their eyes closed in prayer, and yet, in the spiritual world, their eyes were "opened" to see the Lord. As they closed their eyes in prayer, their eyes were opened in prayer to see the greatness of their God. They were encouraged by seeing him, and it gave them faith to act. And as they responded in faith, God gave one of the greatest victories his people had ever known.

So, yet again, remember our question—what is faith? Faith is gazing upon God in prayer. That is how we express faith. We gaze upon God in prayer. However, faith is also expressed by focusing on God's Word. In John, Chapter 3, Jesus describes faith as the *gaze of the soul*. Nicodemus, one of the rulers of the Jewish people, came to Jesus in the dark of night. He was a good man, a devout man, but with regard to his relationship with God, he had no peace in his heart. Jesus said to him, "Nicodemus, you must be born again." And Nicodemus replied, "How is this possible? How can a man be born again when he is old?" Jesus directed Nicodemus to the Word of God, and this Jewish leader learned a lesson that we need to learn right now—Faith is gazing upon a saving God in his Word.

That is how we find faith—by gazing into the Word of God. What did Jesus tell Nicodemus? We all know the beloved words of John 3:16, yes, but what comes just before verse 16? They are Jesus' words about the way of the new birth.

> *"And as Moses lifted up the serpent in the wilderness,*
> *so must the Son of Man be lifted up, that whoever*
> *believes in him may have eternal life. For God so loved*
> *the world, that he gave his only Son, that whoever*
> *believes in him should not perish but have eternal life."*
> (John 3:14-16)

Jesus directed this religious leader, this very learned man, to the Word of God. The Lord is reminding Nicodemus of the events recorded in Numbers, Chapter 21, describing the plague of poisonous serpents invading the camp of the Israelites because of their rebellion against God.

> *From Mount Hor they set out by the way to the Red*
> *Sea, to go around the land of Edom. And the people*
> *became impatient on the way. And the people spoke*
> *against God and against Moses, "Why have you*
> *brought us up out of Egypt to die in the wilderness?*
> *For there is no food and no water, and we loathe*
> *this worthless food." Then the Lord sent fiery*
> *serpents among the people, and they bit the people,*
> *so that many people of Israel died. And the people*
> *came to Moses and said, "We have sinned, for we*
> *have spoken against the Lord and against you.*
> *Pray to the Lord, that he take away the serpents*
> *from us." So Moses prayed for the people. And the*
> *Lord said to Moses, "Make a fiery serpent and set it*
> *on a pole, and everyone who is bitten, when he sees*
> *it, shall live." So Moses made a bronze serpent and*

*set it on a pole. And if a serpent bit anyone, he*
*would look at the bronze serpent and live.*
(Numbers 21:4-9)

The people were being attacked by serpents. Many were dying, some were already dead, and all were terrified. They cried out in desperation to the Lord, and the Lord responded to them by instructing Moses to make a serpent out of bronze and raise it up on a pole in the midst of the camp of Israel. Every Jewish person who looked to that serpent was healed.

Jesus cited this story and, in effect, said, "Nicodemus, that is how you are born again. You must look. You must believe." Just as the Israelites looked to that serpent, we, too, must look to the Son of God. Once again, Jesus is connecting *believing* and *looking*.

So, once again, what is faith? It is the gaze of the soul on a saving God. And where do we see him? By faith, we "see" God in prayer and "see" God's face in Jesus Christ, who can only be found in the Word of God. "Looking to Jesus" is how we believe. It is how our faith is created.

**"Looking to Jesus" is how faith is created.**

In times of trial of our faith, when we are so susceptible to embracing fear, I challenge us all to look with our eyes on our God by closing our eyes in prayer. Let us confess that there are times when we don't know what to do. But in those times, may our eyes be fixed on Jesus. May we truly *look* with faith into the Word of God. We should not just read it and have our devotions, but may we ask the Lord to help us see him in his Word.

### *WHERE DOES FAITH LOOK?*

We have discussed what faith is and how faith is created, but let us now look at where faith focuses. The answer can be found in the words of Hebrews 12:1-2. Here, we find a beautiful and amazing image of "gazing upon Jesus." Faith gazes upon a saving God, and that saving God is our Jesus. Our faith is created and sustained as we focus on him. We are enabled by the grace of God to gaze upon him. As we gaze on Christ, we discover that he is the source of our faith. I encourage you to look at the phrase again, read it aloud, and listen to your own voice affirming the Word of God.

### "Looking to Jesus, the founder and perfecter of our faith."

The word "founder" is from the Greek word "arxagon." We get our English word "architect" from this source. As we look to Jesus, he is the founder of our faith. So, where do we find faith? We find faith in the founder of our faith. Like an architect, he designs and builds faith in us as we gaze upon him. In fact, the Lord "tears down" the old life and builds us new through faith as we focus our gaze upon him.

The chorus of the old gospel hymn "Turn Your Eyes Upon Jesus," written by Helen Howarth Lemmel, is so true:

*Turn your eyes upon Jesus*
*Look full, in his wonderful face*
*And the things of earth will grow strangely dim*
*In the light of his glory and grace.*

Yes, Jesus is the source of our faith, but he is also the *sustainer* of our faith. We are to look unto Jesus because he is the founder and the perfecter of our faith (Heb. 12:2). "Perfecter" means that he is the completer. Isn't this great news? He has begun this work of faith in us, and he will complete it until the day of Jesus Christ, as Paul tells us in Philippians 1:6.

*And I am sure of this, that he who began a good work in you will bring it to completion at the day of Jesus Christ.*

Jesus will cause our faith to hold fast. He will cause our faith to grow as we look to him, and yet, all the while, it is Jesus himself who sustains us.

In the midst of trials, we are enabled to persevere in the faith. Jesus said, "In the world you will have tribulation. But take heart; I have overcome the world" (John 16:33). In Scripture, our journey is often described as one of hardship and trials. And yet, in the crucible of challenges, our faith holds and is sustained as we focus on the Lord Jesus Christ. He is the founder, perfecter, and protector of our faith. And it is God's grace that causes us to *continue to look* to Jesus. We must remember that faith is not looking once and then looking away. We are called to gaze upon him, to focus our eyes upon him, because our faith must have a focus.

> Jesus Christ is the focus of our faith.

By focusing on Jesus, we are able to persevere in faith because our Lord inspires us. He is the surpassing inspiration of our faith. Why should we follow Jesus in times like this? Why should we *ever* follow Jesus? *Because it is Jesus we get to follow.* He is the pearl of great price (Matt. 13:45). He is the treasure hidden in the field (Matt. 13:44). He is the inexpressible gift of gracious God Almighty (2 Cor. 9:15). He is the lily of the valley, the fairest of 10,000 to our souls. There is no one like him. When we look to him, we come to know him, and as we come to know him, we love him.

## UNHELPFUL WEIGHTS
## & UNHOLY SIN

Our text in Hebrews 12:1 teaches us that looking to Jesus is also the source of our sanctification. As we focus on him and follow him, he helps us to put aside weights and sins that hinder our journey. A weight is something that is *unhelpful*. It may not be a sin, but it is surely not helpful. It holds us down and holds us back. As we focus on the Lord Jesus, and we pray and are in the Word, he will reveal to us the unhelpful things that are weighing us down. But he also helps us to see the things that are actual "sin." Sin is that which is *unholy*. It is not something that is just unhelpful. A sin is actually unholy; it is contrary to God and his nature. Sin is described in this verse as clinging to us. The author refers to sin as a garment wrapped tightly around us. However, by the grace of God, we have the power to strip it off. God, through the gift of repentance, will help us to lay aside everything that is unhelpful and, by his grace, strip off that which is unholy.

Sometimes, we need brothers and sisters to help us as they speak into our lives and challenge us to grow in grace. True friends can identify what is unhelpful and unholy. We now have the ability, through the extraordinary resources of social media and networking, to build a community that can encourage each other in our walk with the Lord. We can discuss our trials and tribulations regarding our journey with Jesus Christ with fellow trusted Christians. We are on a journey of following Christ, but we should not travel alone. Aloneness is not good. We need the support of other believers, and they need us.

Ultimately, it is love that keeps us looking to Jesus. However, it is not *our* love but *his* love. It is the love of Christ that holds us fast and sustains us. Not our love for him; his love for us. In difficult seasons, what can keep us *"love controlled"* when so many are *"fear controlled?"* The power of love, Christ's love, enables us to look beyond our present trials and focus on the triumphant joy that awaits us. Jesus himself shows us the way to do this. Although Jesus despised the shame of the crucifixion, it was his focus on "the joy that was set before him" that enabled him to endure the cross. Jesus saw an all-surpassing joy. Not the joy of the cross. The cross was terrifying and horrible to him, but he went to the cross anyway for the joy that was *beyond* the cross. It was for the joy of his Father glorified and the joy of the children of God brought back to the Father. His image-bearers would be restored, and the paradise that was lost would be regained. Jesus saw the result of his death on the cross, and it filled him with joy. Jesus saw you and me, and he saw what we could be if he would go to the cross, and with joy, he did it!

It is love that keeps us controlled in a season of fear. Love. Are you feeling fear right now? Solution—think about the love of the One who wore the crown. Think of Jesus Christ. He *wore the crown* because he *bore our sins*, and when we focus our minds on what he did for us, he fills us with love.

Horatio G. Spafford, the author of these lyrics, captures the essence of this joy so well in the song "It Is Well With My Soul."

> *My sin—oh, the bliss of this glorious thought!—*
> *My sin, not in part but the whole,*
> *Is nailed to the cross, and I bear it no more,*
> *Praise the Lord, praise the Lord, O my soul!*

It can be well with your soul today if you look to Jesus Christ. Gaze upon Christ in faith, and it will be well with your soul. You will be completely healed. You may feel the poison of sin in your veins, but if you look to Jesus, he will be your Savior. When he gave his life for you, he was lifted up. Look to him and be saved. Look to the Lord Jesus Christ, brothers and sisters, and be convinced once again that he is worth it. He is the founder and the perfecter of our faith. Yes, there are times when we don't know what to do, but we can pray to him and say, *"Our eyes are fixed upon you, Lord. Take us through the valley."*

As we gaze upon the Lord in prayer and the Word, he gives us faith, sustains our faith, and captures our hearts in love. Take a moment to re-ignite your heart in faith and love by reading aloud the gracious gospel truth from Hebrews 12:2:

> *Looking to Jesus, the founder and perfecter of our faith, who for the joy that was set before him endured the cross, despising the shame, and is seated at the right hand of the throne of God.*

### PRAYER

*Lord, we ask for your grace to sustain us. Thank you for beginning the work in our hearts and bringing us to see the glory of God in the face of Jesus Christ. Oh Lord, help us to fix our eyes upon Jesus. And Lord, fill us with your love so that, come what may, we will follow our Lord and Savior Jesus Christ. Thank you that wherever he leads us, he leads us in love, mercy, strength, truth, and grace. Thank you, Jesus, that you are leading us home.*

*Amen.*

# R.E.A.P. GUIDE

**R**EAD
- Read Hebrews 12:1-2.
- What do you think the Holy Spirit intends to teach us from this passage?

**E**XAMINE
- "Therefore" (12:1) connects those in the Hall of Faith (Heb. 11) to all followers of Jesus who walk by faith with him today. How are the faithful in Hebrews 11 described in this verse? In what way do they encourage believers today?
- What are the two commands beginning with "let us?"
- What type of race is *living by faith* compared to what is described in verse 1?
- How is sin described in verse 1? How does sin "cling so closely" to believers?
- Believers are commanded to run the race by "looking to Jesus" (12:2). Reflect on all that you have learned about Jesus and the encouragement believers have by looking to him.

**A**PPLY
- The Lord Jesus endured so much for his people! Have you been tempted to focus on your problems, whether they be small or big? What will you focus on about the Lord Jesus to help you have faith through your difficulties?
- In what ways do you see sin "cling so closely" to you and those around you during times of great challenge? What help do *you* need, and what help can you commit to being for others?

- In times of personal hardship, we need to see beyond ourselves and our unique challenges. Considering the reality of persecuted believers and the cause of witnessing for Christ, what types of prayer requests should we be praying for ourselves and others?

PRAY
- Using the "PRAY" acronym, respond with **P**raise to the Lord, **R**epent of sins that this Bible passage has revealed to you, **A**sk the Lord for any requests you may have, and **Y**ield to his will.

# - 3 -

# Is Good Friday Good?

*Then the soldiers of the governor took Jesus into the governor's headquarters, and they gathered the whole battalion before him. And they stripped him and put a scarlet robe on him, and twisting together a crown of thorns, they put it on his head and put a reed in his right hand. And kneeling before him, they mocked him, saying, "Hail, King of the Jews!" And they spit on him and took the reed and struck him on the head. And when they had mocked him, they stripped him of the robe and put his own clothes on him and led him away to crucify him.*
(Matthew 27:27-31)

"Is Good Friday good?" That is the question I asked of the congregation when I began my message on April 10, 2020, just 42 days after the first confirmed death of the coronavirus. On that holy weekend, hundreds of millions of believers worldwide could not gather in houses of worship. Thousands of people had been separated from loved ones who were in hospitals and care facilities. Grieving families were unable to mourn and bury their dead together. Schools closed, businesses shuttered, and playgrounds were empty. Countless individuals had their lives turned upside down in so many different and difficult ways.

Throughout that challenging time, I prayed with many brothers and sisters in Christ, members of my own church family, who were grieving the passing of their dear family members. In seeking some time of solitude, I recall walking through a cemetery and passing a child-sized coffin sitting alone, ready to be lowered into the ground. Undoubtedly, it was a tough and troubling time unmatched by the current generation. So, again, let me ask you, "Was that Good Friday good?"

In a world currently facing so many sorrows and sufferings on so many fronts, what could possibly make any Good Friday good? Only one thing, and that, my friend, is the reality of the One who wore the crown on *that* first Good Friday and every day since. So, the answer to the question is, "Yes, *that* Good Friday and every Good Friday is surely good!"

As we consider these verses in Matthew, Chapter 27, let us focus on the *Crowned One*—the One who was victorious over death and sin on that first Good Friday. The One who finished the work that the Father gave him to do. As we read this chapter, let our thoughts be drawn to him. Let us think about the *crown* that he wore. If we take some time to reflect on what Jesus did that day, nearly 2,000 years ago, we can know, despite all things, that yes, every Good Friday is good.

## THE CROWN OF SCORN

The crown that Jesus wore was a crown of thorns, but it was intended as a *crown of scorn*. Into the mind of one of those Roman soldiers came the idea to devise the ultimate scorn of shame that they could place on the head of the One who claimed to be the King of the Jews. However, that sinister scheme did not begin in the heart of that Roman soldier. Oh, no. That scheme began in the depths of the fiend of hell himself—Satan—who hated the Lord Jesus Christ with all his might. The soldiers laughed as they scoffed, slapped, and spit upon the King of the Jews, but encircling them as they did this were the howling hordes of hell. They gleefully poured out eons of hatred and venom into the face of the One who was crowned with thorns.

The Roman soldiers hated the Jews. To show their disgust for being stationed in Jerusalem (a godforsaken place), they laughed in cruel mockery, bent their knees, bowed their heads, and pledged their loyalty to the king of the Jews. But their words and actions were completely unattached to their wills. They would never surrender their will to Jesus, so they sarcastically placed a crown of scorn upon his head instead.

In a much more subtle and "respectable" way, there are millions, still to this day, who place the crown of scorn on the brow of Jesus. These are people who honor Jesus with their lips, but their hearts are far from him (Matt. 15:8). God forbid that there would be some people reading these pages who would be numbered with those Roman soldiers. That sin would be far greater than that of the soldiers who scorned Jesus in their disbelief and their lack of understanding. How much more grievous is the sin of those who *know* Jesus to be Lord yet stubbornly and consistently refuse to surrender to him?

But God be praised that the One who bore the crown of scorn still has a heart that beats with compassion and mercy, and whose prayer was, "Father, forgive them, for they know not what they do" (Luke 23:34). Thank God for such a king who, though he was so scorned, yet in his amazing grace still freely forgives those who, like the centurion, will say from their heart, "Truly this [is] the Son of God" (Matt. 27:54). Yes, we can declare that Good Friday is good because Jesus willingly wore the crown of scorn placed on him by the Roman soldiers.

### THE CROWN OF SUBSTITUTION

That crown was also a *crown of substitution*. Jesus did not deserve this crown, yet he wore it in the place of one who was called Barabbas. In Matthew 27:16, the Bible tells us that a notorious, infamous prisoner named Barabbas was on the top of the Sanhedrin's most-wanted list. In Judea, Barabbas was public enemy number one. Barabbas was feared and hated by his own people and also by the Romans.

Other gospel accounts tell us that Barabbas was a murderer and a robber. Jesus wore the crown that Barabbas so completely deserved because Barabbas was the king of the criminals. Barabbas deserved the crown. But on that first Good Friday, Jesus wore Barabbas's crown. It was Barabbas's scourging that Jesus endured. It was Barabbas's cross that Jesus bore. It was Barabbas's spikes that pierced Jesus' body. It was Barabbas's execution that Jesus endured. Jesus was Barabbas's substitute. Jesus died in that sinner's place. Was it Good Friday? Not for Jesus. But it certainly was Good Friday for Barabbas.

For a moment, let us take a closer look at Barabbas. Doesn't he look somewhat familiar to you? Haven't you seen him before? Take a good look at him, and then take a good look at his name. His name is Barabbas, or Bar-Abbas, which means "son of the father." Did any son ever dishonor his father's name more terribly than Barabbas?

But Barabbas was an image-bearer. He was made in the image of God. He was made in the likeness of the Lord, but Barabbas wasted his entire life living in rebellion against the

One whose very image he bore. He hated the One who would give his life for him. Who more justly deserved condemnation and execution? But it did not happen to Barabbas because someone had taken his place. Who did that? We know who did that—Jesus. My friend, Jesus, is the true Barabbas. He is the true "Son of the Father." He is *the* Son of God.

Each one of us could benefit greatly by taking a closer look at Barabbas because, in so many ways, he is more than familiar. If we have the courage to look, we will find that, in reality, Barabbas is identical to *us*. As a matter of fact, each of us is Barabbas. I am Barabbas and you are Barabbas. We are made in the image of the Father. We bear the likeness of the Lord, but each of us has been robbers of our own birthright. We have rebelled against our Heavenly Father and are murderers of his Son who was crucified for our crimes.

Yet, *it was* Good Friday because it was the injustice of Jesus' execution that satisfied the justice of God upon our sin. It was the injustice of Jesus' execution that God used to execute his justice that was so due upon *our* sin. It was through amazing grace that, by his stripes and wounds, we have been healed (Isa. 53:5). The "heavenly Barabbas," the true Son of the Father who died, willingly exchanged his life, the just for the unjust, that he might bring us to God (1 Pet. 3:18). Jesus, the true Barabbas, took our place so that we might be set free from death row. And we might become the heavenly Barabbas. Jesus died for us so that we could become true sons and daughters of the Father now and forevermore. Yes, it was Good Friday because Jesus wore the *crown of substitution*.

Events that occurred on that first Good Friday had never been more wrong. The arrest was wrong. The trial was wrong. The interrogation was wrong. The torture was wrong. The judgment was wrong. The execution was wrong. The murder was wrong. It was all wrong. But...it was *all right*. It was all completely right in the sovereign plan of God because *Jesus was completely in control.* His crown of thorns was a crown of sovereignty.

## THE CROWN OF SOVEREIGNTY

If we had been there the night that Jesus was so abused or the day that Jesus was nailed to the cross, we would have thought that things were completely out of control. But throughout this shameful ordeal, as Jesus wore that crown of thorns, he also wore the *crown of sovereignty.* Jesus was in complete control. He was in control of all of the events that night and all of the events that morning.

Jesus was not on trial. In reality, mankind was on trial. Jesus was put under oath. The high priest challenged him by an oath to testify whether he was the Son of God, and Jesus rightly and truly declared that *he was.* He was interrogated by that prideful coward Pontius Pilot, who asked him, "Are you a king?" Jesus answered, "My kingdom is not of this world. If my kingdom were of this world, my servants would have been fighting, that I might not be delivered over to the Jews. But my kingdom is not from the world" (John 18:36). Jesus is the King, but his kingdom is not of this world.

You see, Jesus was in control that day. He was in control of events, but he was also in control of *himself.* By his own testimony, he could have asked the Father, and thousands of legions of angels would have come to his rescue, but Jesus did not ask for angels to deliver him. He begged for strength to do the will of God.

**Jesus *wanted* to do God's will.**

Jesus was in control of himself. He did not return accusation for accusation. Even as he was abused, Jesus did not defend himself. He committed himself to the One who judges righteously.

Jesus also did not reject the pitiful cry for mercy from the criminal hanging beside him on the cross. The same criminal who had ridiculed Jesus and cursed him moments before, by God's grace, suddenly recognized Jesus as the Messiah. Hanging there beside him, he begged, "Jesus, remember me when you come into your kingdom." And Jesus replied, "Truly, I say to you, today you will be with me in paradise" (Luke 23:42-43). Jesus was in control.

Jesus' life was not taken. No one took Jesus' life. Jesus laid his life down willingly for sinners like you and me. Jesus was in total control. It was Good Friday, and when everything was wrong, when nothing made sense, and when it was truly the world's darkest hour, Jesus was in control. Nearly 2,000 years later, Jesus is still in control. He wears the crown, and it is the crown of absolute sovereignty. Life is not always good, but Jesus always is.

**Life is not always good, but Jesus always is.**

And *in* him and *through* him, it can always be Good Friday. In Jesus Christ our Lord, who has conquered death for us, who lives on our behalf, and who is coming for us one day, *every day* is Good Friday. May we worship this wonderful crowned Lord even as we study his Word and give him thanks.

Friends, when we experience life's storms, we sometimes feel separated from God's love. But during dark seasons, we can thank our blessed God that he is in all places, at all times, and we are never, ever alone.

We are never, ever alone.

## PRAYER

*Sovereign Lord, we thank you that you never leave us or forsake us. We praise your name for what you accomplished through your Son on Good Friday—the momentous event that truly made every day a "Good Day" for us, your redeemed children. On that darkest of all days, you sent out the light of your salvation to the ends of the earth. We praise you, O, Lord, for the moment in each of our lives that you shined your saving grace into the darkness of our hearts and caused us to see the light of the knowledge of your glory in the face of Jesus Christ. Jesus, may the radiance of your face always be before us as we journey through the dark seasons of life. May you brighten our path through the light of your Word. May our minds be forever fixed on you through faith. And may we always and only worship you, our Savior, King, and living Lord, Jesus Christ.*

*Amen.*

# R.E.A.P. GUIDE

READ
- Read Matthew 27:11-31.
- What do you think the Holy Spirit intends to teach us from this passage?

EXAMINE
- On Palm Sunday, we remember the event when Jesus rode into Jerusalem on the back of a colt. People cried, "Hosanna," which means, "Save now, we pray!" On this day, the people honored Jesus as a king. How different is this scene of Jesus' life compared to just a few days later in Matthew 27?
- As Jesus stood trial before Pilate, what question was he asked (11)? His answer, "You have said so," was used to put the burden of the answer back on the questioner. Why did Jesus do this?
- Verses 15-26 describe the scene of Jesus and Barabbas. How is Jesus described, and what happens to him in this scene?
- Verses 27-31 tell of the mockery Jesus endured, the public shame, and the abuse. For what in particular were the soldiers mocking Jesus? What is the irony here?
- Read in conclusion Revelation 19:11-16. The image of Jesus has changed dramatically. How is he described here?

APPLY
- What are your personal takeaways from these accounts of the life of Jesus?
- What message can we apply from these texts to the difficult circumstances we face today?

**P**RAY

- Using the "PRAY" acronym, respond with **P**raise to the Lord, **R**epent of sins this Bible passage has revealed to you, **A**sk the Lord for any requests you have, and **Y**ield to his will.

# - 4 -

# THE CONQUEROR OF DEATH

*I, John, your brother and partner in the tribulation
and the kingdom and the patient endurance that are
in Jesus, was on the island called Patmos on account
of the word of God and the testimony of Jesus. I was
in the Spirit on the Lord's day, and I heard behind me
a loud voice like a trumpet saying, "Write what you
see in a book and send it to the seven churches, to
Ephesus and to Smyrna and to Pergamum and to
Thyatira and to Sardis and to Philadelphia and to
Laodicea." Then I turned to see the voice that was
speaking to me, and on turning I saw seven golden
lampstands, and in the midst of the lampstands one
like a son of man, clothed with a long robe and with a
golden sash around his chest. The hairs of his head
were white, like white wool, like snow. His eyes were
like a flame of fire, his feet were like burnished*

*bronze, refined in a furnace, and his voice was like the roar of many waters. In his right hand he held seven stars, from his mouth came a sharp two-edged sword, and his face was like the sun shining in full strength. When I saw him, I fell at his feet as though dead. But he laid his right hand on me, saying, "Fear not, I am the first and the last, and the living one. I died, and behold I am alive forevermore, and I have the keys of Death and Hades.*
(Revelation 1:9-18)

I vividly recall what a strange and different Easter was observed in 2020. Many church buildings were empty that day because of concerns regarding the coronavirus. Regardless, it was still a wonderful Easter because even though church buildings were empty, our hearts were full because our Lord's tomb was empty. Ultimately, it is the empty tomb of Jesus that fills the worship of his followers with living praise. Despite the trials, the truth remains the same—Jesus is alive! Jesus is alive, and no virus can infect or weaken our praise to the One who wears the crown. Jesus is the victor because he has overcome sin, death, and Hades, and he is alive forevermore!

That same living Christ illumines all our darkness, just as he illuminated the cave of Apostle John, who was imprisoned on the Isle of Patmos. He was banished there because of his faithfulness to the gospel and his testimony for Jesus Christ. The Roman emperor Domitian believed that this old man in his mid to late 80s was finished; his ministry would no longer be a threat to the peace of the empire, and before long, he would be dead, worked to death in the mines of Patmos.

But that was far from the case. Perhaps the greatest ministry of Apostle John was granted to him when he wrote, from banishment on Patmos, the words contained in our Bibles as the Book of Revelation. John was imprisoned, yes.

His cell was tiny, but his dark cave was illuminated when he saw his Master, the *Conqueror of Death*. By the Spirit's grace, I pray that we see Jesus afresh and anew in the light of his revelation in this passage as the One who remains the conqueror of death.

## *JESUS IS THE LORD OF GLORY*

When Jesus manifested himself to John in that cave, how different he appeared; Jesus revealed himself to John as the Lord of Glory. We are told of the incredible impact on John when he sees his beloved Savior in all his majesty. John fell at Jesus' feet as though he were dead. His own testimony in Revelation 1:17 is, "When I saw him, I fell at his feet as though dead." How amazing that is! Think of it; this is Apostle John. This is the disciple who was closest to Jesus. This is the disciple who laid his head on Jesus' chest at the Last Supper, the night before our Lord was crucified. This is the disciple who is called of all the disciples—*the disciple whom Jesus loved*. This is the disciple, so close to Jesus that in Jesus' dying moments, he entrusts him with the care of his mother. John knew Jesus. He *really* knew Jesus, yet in his presence, when John sees Jesus in all of his glory, he collapses before him like a dead man.

When John saw the glorified Christ that day, he beheld the unveiled Deity. That word *unveiled* is important. It actually is the meaning of the word *revelation*. This last book in our Bibles is titled The Revelation of Jesus Christ, but the words actually mean *the unveiling of Jesus Christ*. In the words of this final epistle written by the last of the apostles, Jesus Christ is unveiled in all of his eternal glory.

When John looks at Jesus, he sees him as having eyes shining with the fire of omniscience. He hears him with a voice that is resounding with the power of omnipotence. He sees him with hair not brown as a young man but gleaming white with the years of eternity. John sees Jesus with feet blazing with the purity of justice and judgment.

You see, the veil of time and space had been lifted and unveiled before John was the Great I Am, the Lord of Glory, the Prince of Life. For John, it was just too much; he collapsed like one who had been struck dead.

However, this experience reveals something else to John. He not only sees Jesus in his unveiled deity but also *sees himself* in his *unworthy humanity*. John collapses before the unveiled deity as a sinner struck down by God's awesome holiness because he is able to see himself clearly in his unworthy humanity.

Now, remember, John is in his late 80's. He is a good man; there was none better than John. He is a godly man who loves the Lord Jesus with all his heart, soul, mind, and strength. John has been a faithful servant of Jesus since the days of his youth—for at least 65 years. But before the risen Lord of Glory, John is so overcome by the consciousness of his own insignificance and the awareness of his own sinfulness that he falls at the feet of Jesus like a dead man.

Throughout the Bible, we see this repeated. Those who knew the Lord most intimately were awe-struck when they actually saw him in his majesty. Let's reflect on the response of some of the individuals and their own "close encounter of the divine kind." Consider Daniel, for instance. When Daniel saw the Son of Man, he said, "I was frightened and fell on my face" (Dan. 8:17). Isaiah had a similar experience when in a glorious vision he beheld the Lord of Glory and cried out, "Woe is me! For I am lost; for I am a man of unclean lips, and I dwell in the midst of a people of unclean lips; for my eyes have seen the King, the Lord of hosts!" (Isa. 6:5).

When Elijah, the great prophet, heard only the *whispering* voice of Jehovah in that cave, he wrapped himself in a cloak and covered his face. Abraham was known as the friend of the Lord, yet in the Lord's presence, he confessed, "Behold, I have undertaken to speak to the Lord, I who am but dust and ashes"

(Gen. 18:27). And consider Peter, the leader of the disciples. When he understood the Lord of creation was in his fishing boat, "he fell down at Jesus' knees, saying, 'Depart from me, for I am a sinful man, O Lord'" (Luke 5:8). Yes, the people who knew the Lord best were at times overwhelmed in his presence.

This reminds me of a saying often repeated by wheat farmers in the mid-west, "The head of wheat that is the fullest bends the lowest." The mind that is filled with the glory of the Lord Jesus Christ will bend very low in his presence. The person who truly knows Christ knows him for who he is and also knows his own place in comparison. A person who truly knows the Lord Jesus Christ knows that next to Jesus, his or her own place is a place of humility, worship, and adoration. In the presence of the Lord Jesus Christ, the only place we belong is at his feet. Brothers and sisters, may that be *our* place. If it has not been our place recently, may it be our place today. Right now. May we come, once again, humbly before the Lord Jesus Christ.

### JESUS IS THE LORD OF GRACE

Sixty years had passed since John had seen Jesus, and now, in a matter of moments, he comes face-to-face with the Lord of Glory and falls at his feet as dead. Then occurs one of the most beautiful, touching things recorded anywhere in Scripture. While this old, gray-haired man was bowed like a dead man before the feet of the Lord of Glory, Revelation 1:17 says, "But he laid his right hand on me, saying, 'Fear not.'" Gray-headed old John lies prostrate before the Lord and then feels a touch. It is a touch that he has not felt in over 60 years, but it is a familiar touch to every fiber of his being. It is the touch of his Master's hand. He remembers that touch, and he hears that voice, and yes, it is a majestic voice, but in its majesty, it is warm and gentle. It is the voice that he remembers so well, the voice of his beloved friend, Jesus, that says to him, "Fear not."

What a wonderful truth for us to claim today—the truth that our Savior Jesus Christ is the Lord of Glory. Yes. He is the risen One. But he is also the Lord of Grace. "Fear not," is what Jesus said. "Fear not" is still the message of the Lord of Glory. Those words told John something he needed to know so desperately—that the *sovereign* Lord Jesus was the same Lord Jesus. *He was still the same.*

> Jesus is still the same.

The Jesus we read about in the gospel is *still the same*. He has not changed. Yes, he has changed in the outward display of his glory, but his nature has not changed. His identity has stayed the same. And thank God, his heart has not changed. *He is still the same.* His hands that hold the stars, and they do, are the same hands that touched the leper. His hands are the same hands that blessed the children. And his nail-scarred hands that are omnipotent are the same hands that were nailed to the cross for you and me.

His eyes do flame with omniscience, but they are the same eyes that wept over Jerusalem and the same eyes that tenderly looked upon his disciples. His feet, which are like fiery brass, are the same feet that staggered and stumbled up the hill of Calvary and to the cross. He is still the same. Lord Jesus is still the same yesterday, today, and forever. Praise God for that! And his message is still the same. It is still the same to us today as it was to John on the Isle of Patmos—"Fear not." What a great and wonderful promise for us to celebrate, not only on Easter Sunday but every day of the year—Fear not!

*We do not need to fear life* because Jesus says, "I am the first and the last, and the living one. I died, and behold I am alive forevermore" (Rev. 1:17-18). As Christians, we do not have to be overcome with fear in life because we have a Master who has overcome death and lives forever. He tells us, "Fear not." His everlasting arms protect us. His everlasting presence pacifies our troubled hearts. His everlasting intercession before his Father pleads for us even now. We need not fear life. *We also do not need to fear death.* Jesus told John, "Fear not, I have the keys of Death and Hades" (Rev. 1:18). A key symbolizes authority. Jesus is saying, "I have authority over death." Our Lord has authority over death because he *conquered* death. Jesus alone wears the crown of ultimate victory because he conquered death by his resurrection and took away the key from Satan, the prince of death. For Jesus' followers, the door of death holds no fear because the master holds the key to that door of death, and he says, "Fear not." We do not have to fear life and we do not have to fear death. And, because of the Lord Jesus, *we do not have to fear eternity.*

**We need not fear life, death, or eternity.**

Jesus said, "I have the keys of Death and Hades." In the Bible, Hades is the dwelling place of the spirits of those who have died. And by his resurrection, Jesus opened the door of eternity to grant eternal life to all who would trust in him. Since Jesus holds in his hand the keys of Hades, we can claim the promise of Apostle Paul, who said that to be absent from the body is to be present with the Lord (2 Cor. 5:8). Death has been defeated, and the grave has been conquered.

*Behold! I tell you a mystery. We shall not all sleep, but we shall all be changed, in a moment, in the twinkling of an eye, at the last trumpet. For the trumpet will sound, and the dead will be raised imperishable, and we shall be changed. For this perishable body must put on the imperishable, and this mortal body must put on immortality. When the perishable puts on the imperishable, and the mortal puts on immortality, then shall come to pass the saying that is written:*

*"Death is swallowed up in victory."*
(1 Corinthians 15:51-54)

When we die or when Jesus comes for us, "We will always be with the Lord" (1 Thess. 4:17). What a wonderful promise! That promise was so real to me and my wife, Susan, as she tenderly held her younger sister's hand, Carol. Carol was just 59 years of age but lost her courageous battle with a terrible illness. Susan and I watched as she took her final breath. It was peaceful and beautiful. Carol took her last breath on earth, but her next breath was in Heaven and in the presence of the Lord. Her faith and trust were in Jesus Christ. She knew him. At that moment, she was delivered from her diseased-ridden body and was immediately delivered into the presence of the Lord. She is there today, thank God. We know that with unshakeable confidence because Jesus holds the keys and says to us, "Fear not."

Those keys are keys *of our deliverance* from the power of Death and Hades. This should fill the heart of every single believer today with such great hope and confidence.

However, if you have not been born again, if you have not turned from your sins and trusted in Jesus Christ and experienced the new birth, those keys in the hands of Jesus are not the keys of your deliverance. They are the keys to your doom. The key in Jesus' hand that unlocks the door to eternal life is the same key that locks the door to eternal doom for those who reject him.

Years ago, a warden holding a key in his hand walked into a prison cellblock. He stopped and stood before a barred and locked cell door and stared at an inmate sitting on his bunk. The warden looked like an angel to the criminal because it was the day of his release. With that key, the warden opened his cell door and led the convict to freedom. About an hour later, the same warden came into the same cellblock, carrying the same key, and he stood before the cell door of another convicted criminal. To that criminal, the warden looked like the angel of death because, with that key, the warden had come to open the door and lead the condemned man to his execution. The same warden. The same cell block. The same key. To one, an opened door of freedom. To the other, an opened door to execution.

This same Jesus, who we read about in Scriptures, who is *the liberator* to all who accept him, is also *the executioner* to all who reject him. The door of eternity will close behind them forever and will keep them from the presence of the Lord and the glory of his joy forever. They will reside in a place of eternal doom and punishment for the rest of eternity.

My friend, which will Jesus be for you? Will he be your liberator, or will he be your executioner? You might be asking, "Can you know?" I have been asked this countless times over the many years of my ministry, "Sam, can you really know?" And I can tell you with full assurance, "Absolutely, yes!" You can know that Jesus is your liberator and that he has opened the door to freedom for you now and forever. However, you do not have to take the promise of a preacher. You can take the promise of a prisoner to a jailer. What am I talking about? I am sharing with you what the prisoner, Apostle Paul, promised the jailer at midnight in Philippi when the jailer fell on his knees, pleading, "What must I do to be saved?" And Paul, the prisoner who was free in Christ, said to the jailer, who was in the prison of his sin, "Believe in the Lord Jesus, and you will be saved" (Acts 16:31).

> Believe in the Lord Jesus,
> and you will be saved.

This is the promise of our living Lord, our loving Savior, Jesus Christ. If you will turn from your sin today and trust only in the merit of Jesus Christ who took your place, who died for you, and who rose again for you. If you will put your trust completely in him today, he will set you free. And you will personally experience the blessed reality that when the Son of God sets you free, you are a free man or woman forever and ever. May this be the day of your freedom. Today, Jesus holds the keys, and the door of eternal life is open. The Bible ends with the "open-door invitation" of life in the Lord Jesus.

> *The Spirit and the Bride say, "Come." And let the one*
> *who hears say, "Come." And let the one who is*
> *thirsty come; let the one who desires take the*
> *water of life without price.*
> (Revelation 22:17)

The door is open, and Jesus holds the key. He wears the Victor's crown, having conquered Death and Hades. His victory can be your victory if you will trust in him as your Lord and Savior. Our hope is in Christ alone.

## *PRAYER*

> *Blessed Master, your empty tomb is our treasury*
> *overflowing with assurances that every promise you*
> *have shared with us is true and secure. Because you*
> *live, Lord Jesus, we live now in you and will one day*
> *live with you forever. Sovereign Lord, you are still*
> *the immutable, eternal, omniscient, and omnipotent*
> *Lord of Glory before whom your disciple, John, fell*
> *as though dead. Your holiness is all-consuming, but*
> *we trust in your grace that is all-sufficient. Grant to*
> *us as we humbly kneel before you in reverent*
> *worship that along with John, we may sense in our*
> *spirit the same loving touch upon us and hear you,*
> *our Prince of Peace, sharing those same blessed*
> *words of unspeakable comfort, "Fear not."*

> *Amen.*

# R.E.A.P. GUIDE

**R**EAD

- Read Revelation 1:9-18.
- What do you think the Holy Spirit intends to teach us from this passage?

**E**XAMINE

- John the apostle was a prisoner on the Isle of Patmos. How does John identify with the churches in his introduction (1:9)?
- While worshiping God on the "Lord's Day" (Resurrection Day—Sunday), John hears Jesus calling on him to write down what he hears and send it to the seven churches. How is Jesus described?
- What message does Jesus have for John in verse 17? Why did John need this message? Jesus also said, "I am the first and the last..." What is the significance of this (compare to Isa. 44:6)?
- What are the four things Jesus reveals about himself in verse 18?
- Anyone who holds the "keys" (Rev. 1:18) has the authority over that person or thing. The keyholder determines who gets in and who gets out. Since Jesus has authority over Death and Hades, how does that apply to believers in Jesus now (see Rev. 1:5)?

**A**PPLY

- How do you view the Lord Jesus? When does he seem most distant to you? When does he seem nearest? How does this passage reassure us about Jesus' connection to his people?
- What fears do you deal with in your everyday life? Death and Hell are the most significant threats we will ever

face. How has Jesus dealt with our most significant threats? How should that influence our thinking and outlook today?

**P**RAY

- Using the "PRAY" acronym, respond with **P**raise to the Lord, **R**epent of sins this Bible passage has revealed to you, **A**sk the Lord for any requests you have, and **Y**ield to his will.

# - 5 -

# FACING THE FOE OF
# OUR FEAR

*Now when David and his men came to Ziklag on the
third day, the Amalekites had made a raid against
the Negeb and against Ziklag. They had overcome
Ziklag and burned it with fire and taken captive the
women and all who were in it, both small and great.
They killed no one, but carried them off and went
their way. And when David and his men came to the
city, they found it burned with fire, and their wives
and sons and daughters taken captive. Then David
and the people who were with him raised their voices
and wept until they had no more strength to weep.
David's two wives also had been taken captive,
Ahinoam of Jezreel and Abigail the widow of Nabal
of Carmel. And David was greatly distressed, for the
people spoke of stoning him, because all the people*

*were bitter in soul, each for his sons and daughters.*
*But David strengthened himself in the Lord his God.*
*And David said to Abiathar the priest, the son of*
*Ahimelech, "Bring me the ephod." So Abiathar*
*brought the ephod to David. And David inquired of*
*the Lord, "Shall I pursue after this band? Shall I*
*overtake them?" He answered him, "Pursue, for you*
*shall surely overtake and shall surely rescue."*
(1 Samuel 30:1-8)

I n March 1933, Franklin D. Roosevelt was just three lines into his inaugural address when he made the statement that, in many ways, would define his vision for his administration. And perhaps even more importantly, this statement would also identify what he considered the greatest enemy and threat to the nation. "So, first of all, let me assert my firm belief that the only thing we have to fear is fear itself...." When Roosevelt made that statement, America was in the grip of an economic depression that had already lasted over three years. Millions of the nation's citizens were out of work, and their desperate condition was providing fertile soil for the seeds of communism and fascism already growing and spreading over the continent of Europe.

President Roosevelt saw that the greater threat to America, other than the financial crisis, was a crisis of fear and the depression of spirit, which caused many citizens to experience the greatest of all losses—the loss of hope. Hopeless people are a threat not only to themselves, their families, and their communities but also to their nation. "Fear itself" is an enemy that is fearful indeed in its destructive power.

This enemy of fear is especially deadly to people of faith, for living in fear and living in faith is an impossibility. So, as people of faith, how can we recognize the symptoms and experience the cure for the deadly enemy of fear? Thankfully, our Lord in his Word provides for us a historical and timeless lesson in the life of David, both the path into fear and spiritual depression, and also, by means of God's grace, the path into the light and liberty of faith. Let's look at both of these paths by beginning with a humble detour in the life of David, recorded in 1 Samuel, Chapter 27.

Now, every one of us is susceptible to fear; not one is immune to it. But there is the *right* kind of fear and the *wrong* kind of fear. People are more vulnerable to dangerous, wrong kinds of fear when they experience significant fatigue. Physical and emotional fatigue makes us susceptible to fear, which is undoubtedly the case with David. David is exhausted physically from relentlessly fleeing from place to place in his efforts to hide from King Saul, who seeks his life. David is tired, physically and emotionally drained, and being so physically and emotionally depleted, David becomes a prime candidate for fear.

### "Fatigue makes cowards of us all."

George Patton, the great U.S. Army general from World War II, once said, "Fatigue makes cowards of us all." The fatigue of fear, however, does not begin in a person's feet. It doesn't first display symptoms through running away. No, "fear fatigue" first manifests in a person's brain. Notice the progression of the symptoms of fear in David's life. We see the first symptoms in the way he is *thinking*. Fear is causing him to think *in the dark*. We are given insight into this in 1 Samuel 27:1.

> *Then David said in his heart, "Now I shall perish one day by the hand of Saul. There is nothing better for me than that I should escape to the land of the Philistines. Then Saul will despair of seeking me any longer within the borders of Israel, and I shall escape out of his hand."*

Notice that we are told, "David said in his heart." David is talking to *himself*. Someone has wittily said that when you talk to yourself, you are probably having a foolish conversation. Well, David is talking to *himself* and also *discouraging* himself. He is "thinking" himself into discouragement as he attempts to devise his own plan to address a traumatic situation. He carefully tries to figure out an action plan that makes the most sense to him. Proactively, he takes matters into his own hands. The problem is that he is planning *under the influence*, the influence of fear. In his fear, he does not think right, so he comes up with a very *wrong* idea. The root of the problem is that in his fear-driven thinking, he is *robbed of faith*. David's fear caused him to forget the promises of God. This is what fear so often does in the life of the believer.

> Fear can cause us to forget
> the promises of God.

In his fear, David forgets all the amazing promises God has made to him. First of all, he forgets that he has been chosen by the Lord. God sought David and found David. He is God's anointed one to be the next king of Israel. Person after person has promised David that he will be king someday. Samuel, the great prophet, has told David he will be king. His best friend, Jonathan, the son of Saul, has told him, "You're going to be the king someday." His wife Abigail has encouraged him, "I know you will be the king someday." Even Saul, the one from whom David is fleeing, has told him, "David, you are going to be king someday." But fear has weakened David's faith by undermining and discounting God's promises.

## WEAKENED HIS STANDARDS

Not only did fear weaken David's faith, but the weakening of his faith led to the weakening of his standards. His wrong thinking began to infect his life's standards, leading to personal compromise. David's thinking in the dark led him to *walking in the dark.*

## WALKING IN THE DARK

> *So David arose and went over, he and the six*
> *hundred men who were with him, to Achish the son*
> *of Maoch, king of Gath. And David lived with Achish*
> *at Gath, he and his men, every man with his*
> *household, and David with his two wives, Ahinoam*
> *of Jezreel, and Abigail of Carmel, Nabal's widow.*
> (1 Samuel 27:2-3)

Talk about a detour! All the road signs on David's journey read, "Welcome to Gath!" Remember Gath? Gath is one of the chief cities of the Philistines. It is also the hometown of a man by the name of Goliath. Yes, *that* Goliath—the giant-sized enemy of God that David, by the grace of God, overcame in battle. Now, here is David in his fear, thinking so wrongly and being so impacted by his fear that he walks into the land of the Philistines, the enemies of God, and *lives with them!*

## COMPROMISED HIS CONVICTIONS

The infection of fear has compromised David's entire system of his life. The fear causes him to be compromised in four key areas of his spiritual health. To begin, it causes David to compromise his *convictions.* He is still God's man inwardly—in his heart, and he still loves God. But *outwardly,* David has conformed his life to those of the enemies of God. He reasons with himself that it is easier to live like the enemies of God. It is safer to be like them. David has allowed his fears to compromise his convictions, but beyond that, he has also *compromised his influence.*

## COMPROMISED HIS INFLUENCE

His compromise does not just impact himself; it never does. His compromise involves other people, starting with his family. David had taken his family and his friends into the land of the enemies of God. So, his personal compromise now also involves his friends and their families. David, their leader, has led them all into the land of the enemies of God. What a fearful threat lurks in unchecked fear! It caused David to compromise his convictions, compromise his influence, and notice what it did to his soul. Fear *compromised his fellowship.*

## COMPROMISED HIS FELLOWSHIP

*And the number of the days that David lived in the country of the Philistines was a year and four months.*
(1 Samuel 27:7)

What do we know about these 16 months of Philistine living? If you study David's life, you will find that he has yet to write a single Psalm during these 16 months. How could he? How could he write the songs of Zion in such a place as Gath? How could he sing or write Psalms of the Lord while living among the enemies of God, compromising his life and the lives of others? How could he experience joy in his heart? Impossible. For 16 months, the greatest songwriter in history wrote no songs.

He compromised his convictions. He compromised his influence. He compromised his fellowship, and most of all (and maybe worst of all), he *compromised his testimony.*

# COMPROMISED HIS TESTIMONY

> *Now the Philistines had gathered all their forces at*
> *Aphek. And the Israelites were encamped by the*
> *spring that is in Jezreel. As the lords of the Philistines*
> *were passing on by hundreds and by thousands, and*
> *David and his men were passing on in the rear with*
> *Achish, the commanders of the Philistines said, "What*
> *are these Hebrews doing here?" And Achish said to*
> *the commanders of the Philistines, "Is this not David,*
> *the servant of Saul, king of Israel, who has been with*
> *me now for days and years, and since he deserted to*
> *me I have found no fault in him to this day." But the*
> *commanders of the Philistines were angry with him.*
> *And the commanders of the Philistines said to him,*
> *"Send the man back, that he may return to the place*
> *to which you have assigned him. He shall not go*
> *down with us to battle, lest in the battle he become an*
> *adversary to us. For how could this fellow reconcile*
> *himself to his lord? Would it not be with the heads of*
> *the men here? Is not this David, of whom they sing to*
> *one another in dances, 'Saul has struck down his*
> *thousands, and David his ten thousands'?"*
> (1 Samuel 29:1-5)

It is difficult to imagine the complete impact of fear on David's life. He is not just living among the Philistines. We are told in this passage that David has become a *captain* of the Philistines —a leader among them. However, although David has earned a rank among these people, he has not *earned their respect.* What did the Philistines say about David when it came time for battle? They said, "Of all people, what is *he* doing here?" Even the Philistines knew that David should not be there. And you can imagine what *his* men and family are saying? They are probably echoing, *"Yes, what are we doing here? We don't belong here."* David gained a rank, but he was not respected by his enemies or his friends. That is the detour and the destination of compromise. When we compromise our convictions, we are not respected by our enemies, and our friends do not respect us either.

Eventually, the Philistines turned David back. They didn't trust him, so they said, "You can't go." But this Philistine's decision was part of God's plan. God is sovereign; he can use even his worst enemies to carry out the plans he has made on behalf of his people. These enemies of God, the Philistines, carried out God's plan by turning David back. They were instrumental in bringing David face-to-face with the strength of his inner enemy—unbelieving fear. God, in his sovereign love for David, used David's personal enemies and the enemies of God's people to provide a treatment plan for David's spiritual and emotional renewal.

## SITTING IN THE DARK

David's journey into the far country of fear began with "thinking" in the dark, which led him to "walking" in the dark. But now notice the most terrible moment of his life: when David finds himself "sitting" in the dark.

> Now when David and his men came to Ziklag on the
> third day, the Amalekites had made a raid against
> the Negeb and against Ziklag. They had overcome
> Ziklag and burned it with fire and taken captive the
> women and all who were in it, both small and great.
> They killed no one, but carried them off and went
> their way. And when David and his men came to the
> city, they found it burned with fire, and their wives
> and sons and daughters taken captive. Then David
> and the people who were with him raised their voices
> and wept until they had no more strength to weep.
> (1 Samuel 30:1-4)

In these verses, we see David arrive at the awful, final destination on his detour of compromise. This is where his unbelieving and fear-focused thinking has brought him. He returns to Ziklag, the town where he has been living with his men, and along with everyone else, they look forward to rejoining their families. However, while he has been gone, the Amalekites have raided and destroyed the city. David has lost everything—his home, his possessions, his family, and his friends. He has reached his lowest point and sits down in the smoking ruin and rubble of his life. Fear has infected David's mind and now completely devastated his life.

But, thank God, fear had not hindered the Great Physician's treatment plan for David's recovery. The Bible tells us that the gifts and the calling of God are irrevocable (Rom. 11:29) and that God will accomplish his purposes in all those he has called to himself (Rom. 8:28). God called David, and although David devastated his life with the infection of fear, the Great Physician had a treatment plan for his recovery. In fact, it was God who *ordained* the consequences of David's poor choices. However, he did not *cause* David to sin. God is not the author of sin. But God ordained the consequences of David's poor choices so that he would ultimately accomplish God's good purposes.

A ministry friend recently recommended that I listen to a message by the noted pastor, Dr. Tony Evans, Senior Pastor of Oak Cliff Bible Church in Dallas, Texas. The message, dated March 22, 2020, is entitled "Divine Disruptions," and in it, Dr. Evans made a statement that gripped my heart, "God will let things get as chaotic as they need to be until he gets our undivided attention." That is so true. God will do whatever is necessary to get our attention so he can correct our vision.

> God gets our attention so he
> can correct our vision.

59

God often gets our attention through the painful results of the chaos we bring into our lives so that he can correct our vision. In the first chapter of this book, I made an important statement for us to remember: "God, in his providence, allows us to experience trials so that we learn to view the invisible and to value the invaluable."

God wants us to have a clear vision. He wants his people to be clear-sighted and see what is real and what truly matters. God wants us to view what is invisible but real so we can value what is invaluable. And God, at times, allows trials to come into our lives so that he can get our attention and thus correct our vision. He did this for David.

David has reached his *lowest* point, but he has also reached his *turning* point. Like the prodigal son of the Old Testament, even though David has devastated his life (sitting there among the ruin and smoldering ashes of Ziklag) by God's grace, David comes to himself. He regains his senses. Things become clear to him. He *remembers*. He has forgotten for 16 long months but now remembers who he is. And he remembers *whose he is*. He also remembers what he has that cannot be taken away from him. And in that dark moment, David (by God's grace) experiences a fantastic recovery.

What radical new treatment was used to recover David from this illness of fear? It is actually an ancient remedy that has timeless effectiveness. The remedy that worked for David 3000 years ago is the timeless medicine of the Lord that is effective to this day for all of us who are in the dark places of fear. By God's grace, David experienced the healing *power of faith*.

## THE HEALING POWER OF FAITH

Notice how wonderfully the healing power of faith was applied in David's life. Although the healing properties are from the Lord by his grace, David self-administers that grace. The answer and healing are from God, but David self-administers the vaccine that God has provided. Notice that David *encouraged himself* in worship.

### David encouraged himself through the worship of God.

1 Samuel 30:6 is one of the most remarkable verses in the Bible. David sits in the ruin of Ziklag. Without a doubt, he has lost everything. He has lost his family, and now his friends are talking about stoning him. To quote the title of a book my children often asked me to read to them when they were small —it had been a *...terrible, horrible, no good, very bad day.* But notice in 1 Samuel 30:6 what David did on that awful day:

> *And David was greatly distressed, for the people*
> *spoke of stoning him, because all the people were*
> *bitter in soul, each for his sons and daughters. But*
> *David strengthened himself in the Lord his God.*
> (1 Samuel 30:6)

Don't miss that. *"But David strengthened himself in the Lord his God."* David changed his focus. His focus was no longer a *self-focus*. His focus was no longer on the circumstances in his life. This broken man lifted up his eyes to God, and the change of focus changed everything. David stopped focusing on what he had lost and started focusing on what *he could not lose.*

### David focused on what he could not lose.

The Amalekites had stolen his home, yes. They had stolen his possessions, yes. They have stolen his fortune, yes. They had stolen his family, yes. *But they could not steal his God.* They could take everything else, but they could not take away the relationship he had with his God.

This does not mean that David went into denial. This is not denial. David entered into *reality*—the ultimate reality of God.

## The ultimate reality is God.

Regardless of the world's sneering condescension, when you go to God during terrible trials and testing, you are not going into denial. You are going into reality, my friend. And that is how David returned from his long, dark detour. He came back to reality. He came back to his God and his unchanging love and power. He *remembered* that God was still with him.

During WWII, when so many of London's neighborhoods had been devastated by the Nazi's bombings, people's minds and spirits had been deeply impacted. They had nearly lost all hope. On one occasion, someone took a piece of chalk and wrote over the rubble, "*God is nowhere.*" However, upon seeing what had been written, a believer in the Lord decided to make a *slight* change to the message. Taking another piece of chalk, he marked through "*God is nowhere,*" and using the same letters, he wrote, "*God is now here.*" It's the same situation but a very different interpretation and realization. Regardless of the darkness in which we find ourselves, this is the reality—*God is now here!*

> *"Be strong and courageous. Do not fear or be in dread of them, for it is the Lord your God who goes with you. **He will not leave you or forsake you.**"*
> (Deuteronomy 31:6)

This is worth repeating over and over again—God will never leave us nor forsake us. Period. God has not abandoned his people. He has not left us. He is here. *God is now here.* David encouraged himself through the worship of his sovereign God. Then David did something more. *He encouraged himself to worship God, and then he enlightened himself with the Word of God.*

## David enlightened himself with the Word of God.

*And David said to Abiathar the priest, the son of Ahimelech, "Bring me the ephod." So Abiathar brought the ephod to David. And David inquired of the Lord, "Shall I pursue after this band? Shall I overtake them?" He answered him, "Pursue, for you shall surely overtake and shall surely rescue."*
(1 Samuel 30:7-8)

The "ephod" was an elaborate mantlepiece or breastplate worn by the high priest. And on the two shoulders of the garment were two precious stones referred to as "Urim and Thummim." Many Bible scholars believe these words are best translated as *"Lights and Perfections."* The Bible tells us they were used, at times, to make an inquiry of the Lord—to discern God's will. We are not entirely clear on how that occurred, but it is clear David asked for the ephod because he wanted to inquire of God. He wanted to know God's direction.

This is the first time in 16 months David has done this. Had he gone to God 16 months earlier, before deciding on taking *his own path* into Gath, he would have inquired unto the Lord and been guided in God's will. But he didn't. Regardless, God remained faithful, and when David humbly inquired of the Lord, saying, "Should I do this?" God gave him an answer.

In that day, believers used the ephod of God to inquire of the Lord. Today, we do not have the ephod or need the ephod because we have something infinitely better—the Word of God. Yes, we possess the eternal Word of God that is forever settled in Heaven to guide us in the way of righteousness. We go to the Word of God because the Bible reveals the mind of the Lord. In his Word, we not only find encouragement but enlightenment in times when we are afraid.

### The Bible is the revealed mind of the Lord.

> *The law of the Lord is perfect,*
> *  reviving the soul;*
> *the testimony of the Lord is sure,*
> *  making wise the simple;*
> *the precepts of the Lord are right,*
> *  rejoicing the heart;*
> *the commandment of the Lord is pure,*
> *  enlightening the eyes;*
> (Psalm 19:7-8)

There have been times when I have actually felt too discouraged to pray. Have you ever felt that way? Perhaps you have felt too discouraged to read the Bible. One can make an excuse by saying, *"I'm too discouraged to pray. My heart wouldn't be in it. I'm too discouraged to read my Bible. God knows my heart wouldn't be in it."* But that is exactly the point and the opportunity of the Word of God! In times of discouragement, we must do what pastor and author Dr. David Jeremiah calls "spiritual force-feeding." When we don't *feel* like reading the Bible, that is when we need to read it the most! When we don't feel like praying, we absolutely need to pray because that is where and when the Lord will meet us. He will meet us where and when we return to him. We will overcome the deadly spirit of fear by returning to the Spirit of the Living God.

## *DOING THE WORD OF GOD*

Overcoming our fear requires more than just reading or studying the Word of God. It also requires *doing* the Word of God. David encouraged himself in the *worship of God,* enlightened himself through the *Word of God*, and then engaged himself in the *work of God*.

> *So David set out, and the six hundred men who were*
> *with him, and they came to the brook Besor, where*
> *those who were left behind stayed. But David*
> *pursued, he and four hundred men. Two hundred*
> *stayed behind, who were too exhausted*
> *to cross the brook Besor.*
> (1 Samuel 30:9-10)

Notice David's progression in overcoming the enemy of fear. He worshiped, sought the Word of God, received God's instructions, and then *obeyed those instructions.*

My friend, you cannot read yourself out of the spirit of fear, and you cannot pray yourself out. Yes, we certainly must read the Word of God and pray to the Lord our God, but we must also combine prayer and the Word with a personal commitment to *do the Lord's work.* We must obey what the Lord works into our hearts by doing what he instructs us to do.

Years ago, a woman asked if she might counsel with me regarding the emotional challenges she was experiencing. She was suffering under a spirit of discouragement and fear, continuously overwhelmed by life. She never missed a service at our church. She read her Bible, was involved in several Bible studies, and prayed regularly. She also told me that she journaled every day. So, after meeting with her a few times, I asked her if she could bring one of her journals to our next meeting. She brought several notebooks with page after page completely filled. I took my time and carefully read several pages of her spiritual diary and found *myself* becoming discouraged! Sadly, this dear lady had turned her worship time and her time of prayer into a self-absorbed, self-focus. The writings in her journal were all about *her* problems and *her* needs.

The next time we met, I told her I had a homework assignment for her. She was interested, so I continued, "Before we meet again, I want you to go down to the Knoxville Area Rescue Mission and serve at least four hours a week." She asked, "Why?" I responded, "It is because you are so absorbed with your *perceived* problems that you need to go *see* and *serve* some dear people who have *real* problems. As I recall, that was our last session.

How are you going to deal with your fear and your discouragement? A bottle of pills? A bottle of Scotch? A six-pack or six scoops? Endlessly flipping through the TV remote? Emptying a bag of chips? Or maybe by a relentless recording and recitation of all your problems to God? Perhaps 17 more Bible studies on spiritual warfare? Or by creating a mutually affirming network of negativity on Facebook. May I save you some time? All of that will not work.

God's spiritual health plan has a key component, and that key component is, yes, reading the Bible, praying, worshiping God, and attending church regularly. All of these things are awesome, but all of these things that are so critically important will not in themselves overcome the enemy of fear unless you work a plan, which is *a plan to work*. We must implement what we are learning from God if we are going to overcome the enemy of our fears, grow stronger, and stay healthy. It is not the *hearer* of the Word of God who is blessed, but the *doer* of the Word of God who is blessed (James 1:25).

> The doer of the Word of
> God is richly blessed.

David gave himself to God's work. He obeyed, his spirit was revived, and he was set free. David moved from enduring the weakness of fear to experiencing the victory of faith.

## A VICTORY OF FAITH

Across our country, we often hear the cry, "We've got to get the nation back to work!" That certainly is important. We need to pray for our leaders as they try to determine how the economy should be strengthened. Yes, the nation needs our economy to work, but may I remind us of our real citizenship? Our real citizenship is in Heaven. We are citizens of the Kingdom of God. We serve the King, and we are never out of work!

There is always plenty to do as the people of God. There are countless opportunities. And the reward is not just in Heaven. As we focus our lives on doing good, we reward ourselves. God invites us to be "Christian hedonists," as pastor and author Dr. John Piper aptly phrases God's command to live for joy. Or, as a dear missionary friend of mine who is now in Heaven used to say, we "get in on what God is up to." We overcome the enemy of our own fear as we pour ourselves into the lives of others, and in doing so, we bless ourselves.

During the pandemic of 2020, I drove into our church's parking lot, and an older couple pulled up in a vehicle next to me. Rolling down their window, they said, "Pastor Sam, we don't want to bother you, but we forgot it was Saturday and that the church is closed. We have been out grocery shopping and have purchased a few things for Project Jerusalem, the ministry that the church has started to feed the hungry in our neighborhood. We were wondering if there is any way you could let us into the church." I laughed, saying, "Well, I think I may still have a key."

I got out and opened the door to our children's center and gymnasium while the couple opened the back of their car. I was amazed. It wasn't just a "few things." The entire back of their vehicle was filled with groceries! I helped them carry the items into the building, and it was their turn to be amazed when they saw our gym completely filled with food to deliver to our neighbors. When they finished unloading their many bags of groceries, that couple pulled out of the parking lot, rejoicing. They had purchased and provided an expensive load of goods, but they were all the richer, rejoicing in the Lord!

It is believers engaged in the *work* of the Lord who experience the *joy* of the Lord. Right now, whether in a season of poverty or prosperity, let me encourage you to pause for a moment for self-examination.

## A PERSONAL SPIRITUAL HEALTH EVALUATION

Are you exhibiting symptoms of depressing fear? Have you been thinking, walking, and sitting in the dark? Well, my friend, to escape the enemy of fear, you must follow the *guideposts of faith*.

First of all, *engage yourself in worship*. God is still the same. He is still God. He is still here. He still loves you. The things that are going to last for eternity have not changed. Engage yourself in the changeless love and mercy of God. Secondly, *enlighten yourself in the wisdom of the Word of God*. Be guided, not by circumstances, but by the timeless words of Scripture.

And thirdly, *engage yourself in the work of God*. Look outside yourself, look into your neighborhood or community, and think of ways you can be a blessing to those around you. Write some encouraging notes. Call and check on those you think might be sick physically or struggling emotionally. Pray for people on the phone or by text or email. Go grocery shopping and bring bags of goods to people in need. Contribute financially to those out of work or in need of financial help. Be a witness of your faith, and you will find that the God of victory will give you the victory of faith in the midst of your fear.

It is a wonderful and priceless gift to take time out of our relentlessly frantic-paced lives to admit our need for Jesus to him. Let's do that right now.

## *PRAYER*

*Jesus, we need you every hour. Yes, every hour we need you. We humbly confess this even as we come to you at this hour. We need you, Lord Jesus Christ. It is only through you that we are able to conquer the enemy of fear that is filling this world today and often infecting our hearts. Lord, we thank you that we do not have to work "for" victory but "from" victory because of the victory that you accomplished on the cross for us and confirmed in your triumph over the tomb. Lord of the Ages, we praise you that we may call upon you and draw near to you in faith anytime, anywhere. God, you are here. We bless you in Jesus' name.*

*Amen.*

# R.E.A.P. GUIDE

**R**EAD
- Read 1 Samuel 30:1-8.
- What lessons do you see the Holy Spirit teaching you in this text?

**E**XAMINE
- Consider the two contrasting examples of King Saul and David. What have you learned about their situations and each man's response to them?
- What does it mean to "strengthen [oneself] in the Lord his God"? Compare this to 1 Samuel 23:16-17. What is the similar phrase there? How did Jonathan encourage David?
- What step did David take to strengthen himself in God (1 Sam. 30:6-8)?

**A**PPLY
- How are you currently experiencing difficulties?
- Who around you is experiencing the heat of stress and difficulty right now?
- Based on the example of David and following his lead, how can you strengthen yourself in the Lord?
- Like Jonathan, how can you strengthen others in the Lord?

**P**RAY
- Using the "PRAY" acronym, respond with **P**raise to the Lord, **R**epent of sins this Bible passage has revealed to you, **A**sk the Lord for any requests you have, and **Y**ield to his will.

# - 6 -

# THE THERAPY FOR PEACE

*Rejoice in the Lord always; again I will say, rejoice.
Let your reasonableness be known to everyone. The
Lord is at hand; do not be anxious about anything,
but in everything by prayer and supplication with
thanksgiving let your requests be made known to
God. And the peace of God, which surpasses all
understanding, will guard your hearts and your
minds in Christ Jesus. Finally, brothers, whatever is
true, whatever is honorable, whatever is just,
whatever is pure, whatever is lovely, whatever is
commendable, if there is any excellence, if there is
anything worthy of praise, think about these things.
What you have learned and received and heard and
seen in me—practice these things, and the God of
peace will be with you.*
(Philippians 4:4-9)

M any years ago, my family and I traveled back to Findlay, Ohio, where I once served on a church staff to enjoy some time with our friends there. During our stay, I was invited to participate in a church basketball game between the varsity team of the Christian school and a team consisting of members of the faculty and staff. I was excited to be part of this highly anticipated event.

It was quite a game—back and forth. I especially remember a significant moment in the game when I was able to steal a pass and dribble up the court for an easy layup. Well, it would have been easy, except the person from whom I had stolen the ball felt highly motivated to block my shot. However, as I jumped to make the basket, rather than blocking my shot, the other player under-cut my legs and literally sent me into a somersault in the air. I landed on the court on my left arm and immediately knew something was wrong. The pain was terrible. Later that evening, in the emergency room, the doctor informed me that I had fractured my elbow. Since a cast was not an option, he immobilized my arm in a sling and encouraged me to see my physician when I returned home.

A few days later, in Knoxville, my primary care doctor arranged for me to have physical therapy at the Baptist Hospital. When I arrived at the older facility, I found, to my dismay, that the physical therapy department was located in the hospital's basement, but not just the basement, the *sub-basement,* aka "*dungeon.*" As I recall, there were all kinds of instruments of torture displayed down there, and I certainly was not looking forward to what might lie ahead. My fears were alleviated just slightly when a tiny, kind, very cheerful woman introduced herself as the physical therapist. She said, "Mr. Polson, we are going to restore you to a full range of motion in that arm. After all, motion is lotion!"

Well, it did not feel like lotion, but I certainly did experience a full range of *emotions!* As she manipulated my arm, the therapist cheerfully said, "Today, we are going to try for 15 to 20 degrees of movement, Mr. Polson." Within a few minutes, the room felt like 115 to 120 degrees Fahrenheit to me. The perspiration beaded on my forehead because the movement of my arm was so painful. As I recall, I accused that committed caregiver of being a *physical terrorist!*

As I look back on that experience today, I am grateful for that "painful" therapy because, for over 25 years, I have had that full range of motion in my left arm. It has not been stiff or limited in use at all. Physical therapy kept my arm from becoming immobilized and restricted in movement. Likewise, my friend, our Great Physician, sometimes prescribes *spiritual therapy* so that rather than becoming immobilized or restricted by fear, we can know his presence and peace by experience. The Lord wants us to enjoy the liberty of his peace over the limitations of our fears.

God is the Great Physician. He is Jehovah-Rapha, the Lord who heals, who, in his healing process, also rehabilitates us to live lives of greater freedom as we follow the therapy he prescribes. In these verses from the Book of Philippians, God gives us Therapy for Peace. In the previous chapter, we considered his Vaccine for Fear, but God goes beyond just a vaccine. He gives us spiritual therapy that can produce and maintain his peace. Our Lord is the Prince of Peace, and he wants peace to *reign* in our hearts. His therapy regimen for this peace is clearly prescribed in the book of Philippians. As we implement these therapeutic principles, they bring peace to strengthen us in the middle of whatever difficult situation we may be experiencing.

The first principle we must understand is that our Lord has promised the reality of his peace. Peace was the parting gift the Lord Jesus Christ promised his disciples the night before his crucifixion.

*Peace I leave with you; **my peace I give to you.***
*Not as the world gives do I give to you.*
(John 14:27)

Notice Jesus said *"my peace,"* not *"your peace."* And notice further, Jesus said, "I *give* to you." This is not something we earn or achieve. It is a gift. Peace is a *grace gift* from the Prince of Peace, the Lord Jesus Christ. It is important to remember that when Jesus promised us peace, he was not guilty of partial disclosure or false advertising. Jesus was completely honest as he revealed to us something else about peace.

> *"I have said these things to you, that in me you may have peace. In the world **you will have tribulation**. But take heart; I have overcome the world."*
> (John 16:33)

Jesus said, "In the world *you will have tribulation.*" Yes, there may be times when our trials are very unusually severe. In fact, there may be nothing we can compare them to that we have ever experienced before. Yes, our trials may be *unprecedented,* but they should never be *unexpected* because Jesus predicted that our trials would come.

### Our trials should never be unexpected.

Decades later, Peter, who was there that night and heard Jesus share those words, also reminded us that we should not be surprised by trials.

> *Beloved, **do not be surprised** at the fiery trial when it comes upon you to test you, as though something strange were happening to you.*
> (1 Peter 4:12)

As followers of Christ, we should not consider it strange when we go through trials. Trials for the people of God are normal, not abnormal.

Paul, a veteran of trials, wrote this letter to the Philippians, thanking them for their prayerful and financial support. But, remember where Paul is located when he writes this letter to the Philippians. He is a prisoner in Rome. He is in jail...*again*. As you recall, Paul spent a lot of time in jail. In fact, it was in the jailhouse that the church of Philippi had its great beginning. Paul is in jail again, but his attitude is the same as it was at midnight in that cell in Philippi years before, one of *jailhouse joy*.

> *Even if I am to be poured out as a drink offering*
> *upon the sacrificial offering of your faith, I am*
> *glad and rejoice with you all. Likewise you also*
> *should be glad and rejoice with me.*
> (Philippians 2:17-18)

That is so amazing. The authorities could imprison Paul, but they could not imprison his spirit. Even though he was in chains, Paul was a free man because his spirit was free. He was filled with the joy and peace of the Lord Jesus Christ!

Paul writes to the Philippians, who are also experiencing trials and mistreatment because of their faith. Their freedoms are being limited and infringed upon by the governmental authorities, and yet, what was Paul's message to them? Did he say, "You're being robbed of your civil liberties!" No. Paul told them, "*You are being gifted with a sacred identity.*" In our trials, we should not consider ourselves being robbed of liberty but rather being *gifted* with a sacred identity. What is that sacred identity?

> *For it has been granted to you that for the sake of*
> *Christ you should not only believe in him*
> *but also **suffer for his sake.***
> (Philippians 1:29)

Paul tells the Philippians, and us as well, that suffering is a gift. Yes, a gift. With our gift of salvation has come another gift, and that is the gift of suffering for the sake of Christ. It is through suffering and following the Lord through that suffering that we are granted a special identity, a shared identity with Jesus. We are privileged to identify ourselves with Christ when we suffer, and Paul says we should rejoice in that honor.

Paul had been in prison for over two years when he wrote these words. He was unjustly arrested in Jerusalem and put in prison in Caesarea. He was sent as a political prisoner on a vessel to Rome. He was shipwrecked after having saved the whole crew. Now, he is a prisoner in Rome awaiting trial before the emperor Nero. Having experienced all that injustice, it is important that we note what Paul *does not say*. He does not say, "*Pity me.*" Instead, he says, "*Rejoice with me.*" Paul is in prison, but he is at peace. He is experiencing the promised reality of the Lord Jesus—the promised gift that Jesus gives in times of trials—the gift of peace.

The gift of peace is the *ultimate reality*. The Lord promises to each of us, as well, in our own times of trial—a piece of reality, and that is the reality of his peace. It is such a treasure that Paul, who is experiencing this peace, wants the Philippians to share in this peace as well. He wants *all believers of all time* to share in this peace. That is why the Holy Spirit inspired Paul to write this letter—so believers through the ages, when in deep trial, might share in the promised reality of God's peace in their hearts.

## THE PERSONAL REGIMEN FOR PEACE

In Philippians, Chapter 4, Paul explains how we can experience this promised reality of peace. But, it is important to know that we are not neutral in this process. We do not just wait, and then, after waiting, the Lord gives us peace. We *choose* to enter into the process, actively agreeing with the

Lord, which produces his peace. Paul makes a promise about this in Philippians 4:7:

> And the peace of God, which surpasses all
> understanding, will **guard your hearts** and
> your minds in Christ Jesus.

Don't miss that intentional turn of phrase Paul uses. The peace of God will guard your hearts and minds. Then Paul says at the end of Philippians 4:9, "...the God of peace will be with you."

> What you have learned and received and heard
> and seen in me—practice these things, and **the**
> **God of peace will be with you.**

The outcome of this regimen for peace is that the *peace of God* will guard our hearts and minds and that peace comes from the *God of peace* who is with us. You see, peace is simply the manifested presence of the God of peace in our lives. This is the result or outcome that Paul, by the Holy Spirit, wants us to experience.

Now, let's back up and examine the regimen that leads to the outcome of peace. What leads to the peace of God guarding our hearts and minds? And what leads to the God of peace being with us? What is the regimen that leads to experiencing that reality? The regimen that leads to this outcome is based on three things that Paul mentions—*Our Attitude* (Phil. 4:2-7), *Our Attention* (Phil 4:8), and *Our Actions* (Phil. 4:9). Let's begin by focusing our attention on the first of these three essentials for peace—*Our Attitude.*

### OUR ATTITUDE

Our attitude is incredibly important. Motivational speaker Zig Ziglar once declared, "It is your attitude...that will determine your altitude." Paul shares specifics about the attitude we must have as believers to become people experiencing God's peace. In Philippians 4:2-7, Paul shares what I like to call his six "Be" attitudes that lead to peace.

## PAUL'S "BE" ATTITUDES FOR PEACE

### 1. BE UNITED

As Paul outlines this timeless therapy for peace, he also shares a personal message with two members of the congregation in Philippi. Euodia and Syntyche are having difficulty maintaining a peaceful, personal relationship, so Paul speaks to them personally.

> I entreat Euodia and I entreat Syntyche to agree
> **in the Lord.** Yes, I ask you also, true companion,
> help these women, who have labored side by side
> with me in the gospel together with Clement and
> the rest of my fellow workers,
> whose names are in the book of life.
> (Philippians 4:2-3)

Can you imagine being one of those two ladies when the letter of Philippians was first read in the church of Philippi? My goodness, what a moment that must have been! Why did the Holy Spirit inspire Paul to address such a personal situation in this letter? Paul is prompted to do so because there is a lesson here for *all Christians, in all the church, for all the ages.* The lesson is this: we cannot expect to experience peace *within us* if there is no peace *between us.* Peace is not based on acknowledging who is right or wrong but on acknowledging *who unites us.* We make the choice. We can choose to focus on our disagreements, or we can choose to focus on the One who unites us and decide to be of one mind. How is this possible? Paul shares that it is possible because of three words in verse two: "*In the Lord.*" It is possible to be at peace when we can be of one mind *in the Lord.* Peace requires *peacemaking* in the Lord, and it also requires *peacemakers.*

> *Yes, I ask you also, true companion, help these women, who have labored side by side with me in the gospel together with Clement and the rest of my fellow workers, whose names are in the book of life.*
> (Philippians 4:3)

Paul is speaking to someone who is a friend of Euodia and Syntyche. He pleads with this companion to help these women who have served and labored alongside Paul and Clement. These are wonderful women of God. Their names are in the Book of Life. These are born-again ladies who need someone to come alongside them and help them to make peace with each other. They need a peacemaker. Being a peacemaker is directly connected with experiencing peace.

When we determine that we want to be peacemakers between others, we begin to bring peace into our own hearts and lives. Jesus said, "Blessed are the peacemakers." Part of being blessed is having joy and peace in our own hearts. And when we desire not to take sides in an argument but to unite people in the Lord, we will experience the benefits of that peace ourselves. Indeed, "Blessed are the peacemakers!"

The "Be" attitudes that lead to peace are first of all—*be united.* And secondly—*be joyful.*

## 2. BE JOYFUL

> *"Rejoice in the Lord always;*
> *again I will say, rejoice."*
> (Philippians 4:4)

Apostle Paul *commands* us to be joyful. In fact, he commands us *twice:* "Rejoice in the Lord always; again, I will say, rejoice." Paul emphasizes this subject because rejoicing in the Lord exalts Christ. Jesus is our joy, so when we choose to rejoice in him, we are exalting Christ. Joy exalts Jesus.

And then, there is another reason we are urged to rejoice. Rejoicing in the Lord *edifies us*. We build up and strengthen the muscles of our faith when we choose to exercise our joy in him. Yes, rejoicing is a decision based on our determination to do it. Joy is not an emotion that is prompted by the circumstances from without. It is not the same as happiness because the concept of *"happiness"* is connected to the *happenings* in our lives. Joy is rooted in that which is much deeper, spiritual, and eternal. Joy is the result of Jesus and his manifested presence in our lives. I remember, over 50 years later, the song we sometimes sang as children in our opening assemblies in Sunday school, "Joy is the flag flying high in the castle of my heart; for the King is in residence there." Yes, the King of Heaven resides in our hearts as believers. So, Paul tells us to exalt Christ, even in our trials. When we decide to exalt Christ by rejoicing in him, we edify ourselves.

### *3. BE GENTLE*

> *Let your reasonableness be known to everyone.*
> (Philippians 4:5)

The word Paul uses here for "reasonableness" is very unusual and almost untranslatable in English because so many subtleties of expression are included. Synonyms for the word include "forbearance," "generosity," "kindliness," or "mildness." Perhaps the best way to describe this word would be—*sweet reasonableness*. "Let your **sweet reasonableness** be known to all people." A person characterized by sweet reasonableness is kindly dispositioned toward others.

Strangely, though, kindness toward others is a gift that is hard to give away because the people to whom you are being "sweetly kind" tend to give it back. There is a great theological truth that we should be careful to grasp in our spiritual growth with the Lord—people generally treat us the way we treat them!

> People generally treat us the
> way we treat them.

When we practice sweet reasonableness, this virtue becomes its own reward. While scattering the seeds of kindness toward others, we plant some of those seeds in our hearts and eventually reap the harvest of joy. Kindness is a gift that we give to others and also to ourselves. Ultimately, the kindness we give is given back to us in return, and our own spirits are enriched. Amazing. Grace always is.

## 4. BE EXPECTANT

*Let your [sweet] reasonableness be known to everyone. **The Lord is at hand.***
(Philippians 4:5)

Notice Paul says, "The Lord is at hand." This phrase can also be translated as "the Lord is near." There is a difference of opinion among Bible scholars as to which meaning is emphasized in this verse, whether *the Lord is coming or the Lord is near or present.* The truth is that both meanings apply. This verse reminds us that the Lord is coming. No matter how difficult our day may be, it brings us one day closer to the coming of the Lord Jesus or closer to going to be with him. Either way, we are one day closer to Jesus! And what a reason for joy that truly is!

Approximately one out of every four verses in the New Testament refers to the second coming of Jesus Christ. That means 25 percent of the New Testament has some connection with Jesus' return. The second coming of Christ is at the very heart of what it means to be a Christian—to possess a confidant and expectant hope that Christ is indeed coming again. It is our blessed hope, and it brings us joy. We must also remember that as we anticipate the Lord and his coming, it is also true that *the Lord is near.* "*Let your sweet reasonableness be known to everyone. The Lord is near.*" He is present. He is right here. Right now. We are not alone. My friend, whatever you are going through today, whatever you are experiencing— *you are not alone.* The Lord is near. Rejoice!

## 5. BE PRAYERFUL

*Do not be anxious about anything, but in everything*
*by prayer and supplication with thanksgiving let*
*your requests be made known to God.*
(Philippians 4:6)

The following "Be" attitude involves prayer. Paul challenges us to be prayerful because the Lord is near. God is always close enough to hear our prayers.

I remember that my dad had a message plate attached to the front of his car that read, "Prayer changes things." In my mind's eye, I can still see him driving down the road or pulling up at our house with that testimony displayed on the front of the car, "Prayer changes things." Yes, prayer does indeed change things, and one thing prayer changes, according to Paul, is this: prayer changes worry into trust.

Prayer changes worry into trust.

"Don't worry" is Paul's challenge. "Don't be anxious about anything." The grammar Paul uses conveys the idea of stopping and starting. "*Stop being anxious about anything,*" but "*start praying about everything.*" We could say it this way, "Stop worrying about anything and start praying about everything."

Worry robs us of life itself. The reason it is so terrible to live a life that is full of worry and anxiety is that this behavior robs us of our days. The source of the following quote is unclear, but the truth it conveys is crystal clear, "*Remember, today is the tomorrow you worried about yesterday.*" We smile at that quip, but the admonition should grip us. We can worry our lives away one day at a time. Worry is toxic. Worry is poisonous. But, thank God, there is an antidote to worry that Paul prescribes—*prayer and supplication.*

"*Supplication*" means a specific request. In prayer with supplication, we bring specific situations and issues to the Lord. We don't just generalize, saying, "Bless me" and "Bless everyone." No, we ask the Lord for his help in very specific situations or needs regarding our lives or the lives of others.

As we pray and pour out our hearts to God in supplication, we must also remember something else Paul prescribes for our struggles with fear—don't forget to *give thanks*. We must give our problems to God because prayer overcomes worry, but we must also lift our praise to God. We need to exalt our Master for who he is, what he has done for us, and what is ahead for us in Christ. As we take our praise to God and not just our problems, we will find that he will lead us to peace. "*In everything, give thanks.*" Paul doesn't tell us to give thanks *for* everything but to give thanks *in* everything. We can give thanks even for things that are not pleasant.

I remember the story shared about the noted Bible commentator and minister of the 17th century, Matthew Henry, who was once robbed of his wallet. That night, he read in his Bible the statement from verse 6, "In everything give thanks," and he wondered, "How can I give thanks for being robbed?" After a time of reflection and meditation, this is what he wrote in his journal: "Let me be thankful, first, because he never robbed me before; second, because although he took my purse, he did not take my life; third, because although he took all I possessed, it was not much; and fourth, because it was I who was robbed, not I who robbed."

In everything, give thanks. Everything. Paul's "Be" attitudes are the restorative regimen for our souls: *be united, be joyful, be gentle, be expectant, be prayerful,* and finally:

## 6. BE PEACEFUL

*Do not be anxious about anything, but in everything by prayer and supplication with thanksgiving let your requests be made known to God. **And the peace of God, which surpasses all understanding, will guard your hearts and your minds in Christ Jesus.***
(Philippians 4:6-7)

Paul promises a supernatural peace, a peace that cannot be explained. It is a peace that surpasses understanding. This peace cannot *be explained*, but thank God, it can *be experienced.*

My friend, you can experience that peace today through the Prince of Peace, Jesus Christ.

*Therefore, since we have been justified by faith, we have **peace with God** through our Lord Jesus Christ.*
(Romans 5:1)

Do you have peace with God? God has made peace with him possible through the Peacemaker, Jesus Christ. When you trust in Jesus, repent of your sins, and place your faith in Christ, you are justified and declared not guilty by God. Then, the peace of God is made available to you. By God's grace and through faith, you can have *peace with God* right now, which will lead to the peace of God. This moment, turn away from anything else as your hope of peace, for it is a false hope that cannot provide lasting peace for your soul. But the Prince of Peace, Jesus Christ, came to make peace between a holy God and helpless, hopeless sinners. He made that peace through the blood of his death on the cross as a sacrifice to God and a substitute for sinners. Through faith in what Jesus did for you on the cross, you can have the precious gift of peace. Once again, read this declaration and your invitation:

*Therefore, since we have been justified by faith, we have peace with God through our Lord Jesus Christ.*
(Romans 5:1)

I pray that you will know peace in your heart today—peace with God through Jesus Christ our Lord. May God also grant you, as you follow this regimen from Philippians, Chapter 4, and in particular these "Be" attitudes, that you may experience the priceless outcome—*the peace of God, which surpasses all understanding that will guard your hearts and your minds in Christ Jesus.*

## PRAYER TO THE GOD OF PEACE

*Lord, we thank you for this opportunity to open your Word, and we pray as we come to the close of this chapter that we may not become distracted in these sacred moments and quickly move on to other activities. Lord, may you draw us into your presence to respond to your marvelous grace. Heavenly Father, we are not sharing in God's Word through this book by accident but by appointment. And you, Great Physician, have a goal for each of us in this appointment: to experience peace with you through our Lord Jesus Christ—the unexplainable peace that surpasses all understanding. Oh Lord, I pray and ask that you will accomplish that purpose right now in the heart and mind of every reader. In Jesus' name.*

*Amen.*

# R.E.A.P. GUIDE

**R**EAD

- Read Philippians 4:4-9.
- What lessons do you see the Holy Spirit teaching you in this text?

**E**XAMINE

- There is a way to reach the status that Paul says is available in verses 7 and 9, and it involves commands. As believers, we must remember that the commands of Chapter 4 have a context in the good news of the gospel. Look back at Philippians 3:20-4:1. How does Paul summarize the gospel hope we have, and what does he tell us to do?
- What are the commands listed in verses 4-7? Are there any promises connected to them?

**A**PPLY

- Stress, worry, concern, and anxiety result from a lack of peace. When have you experienced those symptoms of no peace in recent days? What kind of things cause you to experience those feelings?
- "Rejoice...again I will say, rejoice!" What do we have to rejoice about, even in tough times?
- What types of things should we be thinking about and filling our minds with keeping with Paul's commands in verses 8-9?

**P**RAY

- Using the "PRAY" acronym, respond with **P**raise to the Lord, **R**epent of sins this Bible passage has revealed to you, **A**sk the Lord for any requests you have, and **Y**ield to his will.

# - 7 -

# THE GUARDIANS OF
# THE MIND

*Finally, brothers, whatever is true, whatever is
honorable, whatever is just, whatever is pure,
whatever is lovely, whatever is commendable, if there
is any excellence, if there is anything worthy of
praise, think about these things. What you have
learned and received and heard and seen in me—
practice these things, and the
God of peace will be with you.*
(Philippians 4:8-9)

I n his book *The Applause of Heaven*, Max Lucado shares a
very interesting story about the infamous robber of the 19th
century, Black Bart.

During his reign of terror between 1875 and 1883, he is credited with stealing the bags and the breath away from twenty-nine different stagecoach crews. And he did it all without firing a shot.

His weapon was his reputation. His ammunition was intimidation.

A hood hid his face. No victim ever saw him. No artist ever sketched his features. No sheriff could ever track his trail. He never fired a shot or took a hostage.

He didn't have to. His presence was enough to paralyze....

As it turns out he wasn't anything to be afraid of, either. When the hood came off, there was nothing to fear. When the authorities finally tracked down the thief, they didn't find a blood thirsty bandit from Death Valley; they found a mild-mannered druggist from Decatur, Illinois. The man the papers pictured storming through the mountains on horseback was, in reality, so afraid of horses he rode to and from his robberies in a buggy. He was Charles E. Boles--the bandit who never once fired a shot, because he never loaded his gun.


Black Bart paralyzed people with fear. Fear was his weapon, and the ammunition was his reputation.

As believers, we have to be very careful that we don't let "Black Bart" get into our heads and rob our hearts. When fear gains entrance inside our minds, it takes control, and when fear takes control, it robs us. Yes, fear robs us of the precious cargo that each one of us is carrying or should be carrying: the precious treasure of peace. Peace is a precious gift that our Lord Jesus Christ has given to us as his disciples.

*"Peace I leave with you; my peace I give to you. Not
as the world gives do I give to you. Let not your
hearts be troubled, neither let them be afraid."*
(John 14:27)

Peace in our hearts and minds truly is a grace gift from the
Lord Jesus Christ. The enemy wants to rob us of this precious
cargo we carry, and he uses fear as his weapon to accomplish
the crime. To keep from being victims of this pilfering of our
peace, we must remove the hood from this bandit and
determine that "Black Bart" has no authority to demand we
give up anything that has been given to us by Jesus. The
enemy's weapon of fear is full of blanks, and we do not have to
yield a single coin from our treasure of peace to him.
Philippians, Chapter 4, provides a manual on how to do that.

Apostle Paul is writing from prison, but in his chains, he
teaches us how to break free from the prison of fear. We can be
*held captive by peace* instead. Regardless of what is going on
around us, like Paul, we can live free from the prison of fear.
Freedom begins in the mind, and in this passage, Paul
challenges us to stop the *mind games* of fear by making sure
that we do not let our minds become *playgrounds* for fear.
Instead, we must turn our minds into *training camps* for
peace.

In writing this manual, Paul maps out a three-fold
regimen for peace of mind and heart. It requires *attitude,
attention*, and *action*. First, we must uphold an *attitude of
peace* (Phil. 4:2-7). Second, we must focus our *attention on
peace* (Phil. 4:8), and third, we must engage our *actions for
peace* (Phil. 4:9).

In the previous chapter, we focused on Paul's six great
"Be" attitudes or qualities for peace. Let's review those quickly:

**Be United** (Phil. 4:2-3)
If we want to be people at peace, we must become
peacemakers ourselves and help others to be at peace.

**Be Joyful** (Phil. 4:4)
We are told to rejoice in the Lord. Apostle Paul commands us twice to be joyful in the Lord because he is the source of our joy.

**Be Gentle** (Phil. 4:5)
"Let your sweet reasonableness be known to all people." We must focus our dispositions toward gentleness, kindness, goodness, and forbearance.

**Be Expectant** (Phil. 4:5)
"The Lord is at hand," which has two implications: 1) *He is close by*, meaning we are not alone, and 2) *The Lord is coming*. No matter what is happening around us, the Lord is *near* and is coming for us. This is one of the reasons we can be so joyful and live in a state of expectancy, knowing that the Lord Jesus Christ is both near and is coming soon. We have the security of his spiritual presence now and the confidence of his physical presence to come.

**Be Prayerful** (Phil. 4:6)
Paul challenges us to stop being anxious about anything and to start praying about everything. In effect, Paul says, *"Bring everything that causes disturbance in your heart to the Lord. Pray about it. Cast your burdens on the Lord. Take your life and all of its difficult circumstances to Christ, determining to stop allowing anxiety to have control of your mind."*

**Be Peaceful** (Phil. 4:7)
Paul intentionally uses a startling contrast, combining the promise of peace with military imagery. *"And the peace of God, which surpasses all understanding, will guard your hearts and your minds in Christ Jesus."* As you read, pay particular attention to this. Paul says,

"The peace of God will guard your hearts and minds..."
What a powerful and unique image. The word for
"guard" that is used here conveys the idea of a soldier
on guard duty. The peace of God will *stand guard*
around our minds.

The ultimate guardian of our minds is God, the Holy Spirit.
The Bible tells us that the Holy Spirit begins his guard duty of
our minds through the miracle of the new birth. He cleanses
our depraved minds with the "washing of regeneration," as
Paul describes it in Titus 3:4-5:

> *But when the goodness and loving kindness of God*
> *our Savior appeared, he saved us, not because of*
> *works done by us in righteousness, but according to*
> *his own mercy, by the **washing of regeneration***
> *and renewal of the Holy Spirit.*
> (Titus 3:4-5)

As believers, we have been subjected to brainwashing, and
we should praise God for this because our minds are
desperately dirty. We have been brainwashed by the washing
of regeneration through the renewing work of the Holy Spirit.
He is now the Great Guardian of our minds. Our minds are
also guarded through the ministry of the Captain of our
Salvation, Jesus Christ. In 1 Corinthians 2:16, Paul shares that
as believers, we now have the mind of Christ through the
regeneration of the Holy Spirit. When we were born again by
faith, this renewing work began. Our minds, which were once
deprived and darkened in sin, have been made new by the
miracle of regeneration. As believers, we have been given
minds alive to Christ, and we can now think God's thoughts
through him.

*"For who has understood the mind of the Lord so as
to instruct him?" But we have the mind of Christ.*
(1 Corinthians 2:16)

This "mind of the Lord" has been granted to us because of our *position* in Christ, but we must put this mind into *practice*. Earlier in this letter to the Christian Philippians, Paul said, "Have this mind among yourselves, which is yours in Christ Jesus..." (Phil. 2:5). "Let" is a word of agreement. By cooperating with him, Jesus Christ functions as the Captain of the Guard of our minds. We, as soldiers of Christ, are also participants in the process of guarding our minds. We have the responsibility to stand at attention, as it were, and stay alert. We must be attentive to our thought life and, therefore, cannot allow our thoughts to wander unchallenged wherever they want. Paul, by the Holy Spirit, is calling us to be on guard duty, to protect our thinking, and to be mentally alert. There is no time for "chilling out on vacation," so to speak. We must be fully engaged, guarding our thoughts with mental attention.

So, if we are called to attention in guarding our thoughts, what are we supposed to be *attentive* to? Paul answers that question in verse 7 when he tells us to guard our "hearts and minds." These words, "heart" and "mind," are synonyms but are not identical. They are synonyms for our inner nature or the spiritual aspect of our being. The "mind" has to do with our volition or how we *think*. Our "heart" has to do more with our emotions—what we *feel* or what we *sense*. Paul is referring to what we often call our *consciousness*. His challenge, then, and that of the Holy Spirit, is for us to stand guard over our hearts and our minds. We must protect both our emotional and volitional consciousness to maintain the peace of God that resides within us.

This call to mentally stand guard and protect the peace of God leads us to an important question. What specifically are we to stand guard against? Scripture is very clear in answering that question with repeated warnings about three infiltrators who want to creep into the camp of our thinking, creating turmoil and robbing us of God's peace. The three members of this squad are *the world, the flesh,* and *the devil.* These three enemies desire to slink into our thinking and overcome our peace by transferring our focus onto things that are not of the Lord.

*The flesh* in the Bible refers to the remaining influence of sin that is still present within us as sinful, not yet fully redeemed human beings. Our peace can be overtaken when we focus on those things that are part of our old pattern of mental processes. This traitorous infiltrator of the flesh is already within us. *The world* refers to the values and vanities of the world system that exists on this planet in rebellion against the Creator. And then there is the devil, the arch-enemy of God and God's image-bearers. *The devil* desires to capture our allegiance by focusing our attention on that which is not of the truth and, therefore, not of God. *The world, the flesh,* and *the devil*—we have to stand on guard against these three infiltrators. They are so deceptive and so very gifted at impersonating our allies, but they are robbers of our peace in the Lord.

## THE PASSWORDS OF PEACE

So, here is the huge question: how can we possibly defend the gateways to our minds against these infiltrators of our peace? We can keep our minds safe by challenging our thoughts with the *passwords of peace.* The Captain of our Salvation has provided us with inspired words to guard the gates of our minds. These passwords identify our thoughts as either *friendly* to our well-being or *threats* to our well-being. It is our duty to test our thoughts by using these passwords of peace that Paul shares with us from Philippians 4:8.

*Finally, brothers, whatever is **true**, whatever is*
***honorable**, whatever is **just**, whatever is **pure**,*

95

*whatever is **lovely**, whatever is **commendable**, if
there is any **excellence**, if there is anything **worthy
of praise**, think about these things.*
(Philippians 4:8)

## TRUE

Paul challenges us to think about those things that are true.
But he is not only referring to those things that are *factually*
true but those that are *faithfully* true as well. *Faithfully true*
encompasses all those things that are in agreement with the
truth of God. We are not to focus our thoughts on things just
because they are *factually* true. In this fallen world, that could
include many factually true topics or issues that would not be
edifying to our hearts and minds. The question to ask then is
this—are these things *faithfully* true? Do these thoughts agree
with the truth of God?

## HONORABLE

Another way of achieving peace is by focusing our thoughts on
those things that are honorable. "Honorable" means *noble* or
*respectful*. The Greeks and Romans highly valued this quality
of mind, which characterized a person who effectively
communicated with dignity and disposition. Honorable
thinking rises above a focus on concepts that cheapen and
devalue life. This level of thinking is not worthy of those
created in God's image.

## JUST

As followers of Christ, we are to focus our thoughts on those
things that are *just*. The word Paul uses here means *righteous*.
So, his challenge is for us to focus our thoughts on that which
is *in harmony and agreement with God's character*. We are to

reject thinking patterns that do not reflect the character of God because they are, by nature, *ungodly*.

## PURE

We are to focus our thoughts on pure things as well. Pure thoughts are *morally clean*, meaning they are not dirty or filthy. So much of today's media is comparable to a sewer flowing with filth. It is almost impossible to escape its stench, but that does not mean we must allow our minds to become septic tanks. By God's grace, we can choose to think about the things in life that are morally clean.

## LOVELY

Think about the things that are *lovely*. The word lovely is unique. In fact, this is the only time this word appears in the New Testament. The primary concept of the word is *attractive*, but it means attractive in the sense that it *prompts love*; it draws love out of the heart. Thinking about things that are lovely or attractive will focus our attention on ideas or objects that draw out the highest qualities within us.

## COMMENDABLE

We are also to think about things that are *commendable*. Something commendable is *highly respected* or *well-thought-of*. Paul is challenging us to set our minds on those things that are admirable and not to settle for a mindset that is satisfied with "average" as its highest goal. We cannot fulfill our Lord's calling to be "the light of the world" with thinking that is common and dull.

Paul could have continued with a lengthy list of qualities for virtuous thinking, but instead, he summarizes other qualities that could join these "guardians of our mind" by commending to us subjects and concepts that are excellent and praiseworthy. *Excellent* means possessing the quality of *intrinsic value*. Paul encourages us to think about anything that is *worthy of praise,* meaning anything that is well-spoken of and deserves to be well-spoken of.

The word Paul uses in his challenge to "think" on these qualities is very important. It is a word that denotes a mind that is *actively engaged* in a subject or object. Perhaps it might be helpful to paraphrase Paul's challenge to us as "*concentrate on these things.*" He is serious about what our minds focus on and wants us to get serious as well. Why would Paul go to such lengths to be so *descriptive* and *prescriptive* about our thought life? Why is he calling us to be attentive and guard our thought life? It is because Paul knows what we all really must know—*our thoughts are the key to our identity.*

It has been well said by insightful people, "You may not be what you think you are, but what you THINK, you ARE."

> You are what you think.

Our thinking process is ultimately expressed in our living process. How we live is always the outworking of how we think. Our thinking is the key to our identity. What Paul has shared in these verses is the wisdom of God communicated by so many of his servants through the ages. In fact, the wisest man who ever lived wrote these words of challenge about guarding our thought life:

*Keep your heart with all vigilance,*
*for from it flow the springs of life.*
(Proverbs 4:23)

Many people protest this by saying, *"Well, we can't help what we think about. That's impossible."* Well, of course, we can help what we think about! How do we know this? *Because God says we can.* God promises us that by the power of the Holy Spirit, we can *determine* what we think about. Through the inspiration of the Spirit, Paul shares with us in this passage the regimen to bring our thoughts under control. In fact, he promises that we can do more than control our thoughts. We can actually renew our thinking processes by actively engaging our minds in these qualities that guard our peace.

The key to implementing this renewal of our minds is not to focus on individual thoughts but rather to focus on the direction of our thinking. Paul is not saying that we will never have bad thoughts but that we don't have to let our minds be *controlled* by those thoughts.

Martin Luther, the great reformer, quipped, "You cannot keep birds from flying over your head, but you can keep them from building a nest in your hair." Yes, we certainly have bad thoughts from time to time, in fact, often. However, Paul is challenging us to create a *renewed environment* in our minds that no longer welcomes destructive thought processes fueled by the world, the flesh, and the devil. We must determine that because we are *new* people in Jesus Christ, our minds will no longer be "home" to our *old* ways of thinking.

Many years ago, a woman came to me for some counseling regarding her marriage. I was somewhat surprised because she had not been married that long. She had married later in life to a man who was a widower. As I talked with her and asked her to share with me what was happening, she said, "Pastor, I love him, and I believe he loves me, but I'm really struggling." I asked her to help me understand the difficulty, and she said, "Well, we were married last year, and then I moved into his house. But Pastor, there are pictures of his former wife everywhere, all over the house, and it is so troubling to me!"

A few days later, I met with her husband and explained his wife's concern. I asked him, "Brother, do you remember that beautiful service you had for your first wife in the funeral home?"

He said, "Yes, certainly I remember that."

I continued, "My brother, you have got to have a funeral service like that *in your home*. Your first wife will always have a special place in your heart, but she cannot continue to live in your home. There is only room for you and your new wife in your home."

The Lord gave that man understanding about the placement of priority his present wife deserved, and he responded to her with such grace and encouragement. A great peace came into their marriage as a change of focus came to the photographs in their home.

Likewise, if we are going to have thoughts that follow the Lord's will, they must be thoughts of our new life in Jesus Christ. And how beautiful that life is!

> *Finally, brothers, whatever is **true**, whatever is*
> ***honorable**, whatever is **just**, whatever is **pure**,*
> *whatever is **lovely**, whatever is **commendable**, if*
> *there is any **excellence**, if there is anything*
> ***worthy of praise**, think about these things.*
> (Philippians 4:8)

Paul reminds us that there is beauty *all around us*. Those things should be the controlling focus *within us*.

## THE BEAUTY IN GOD'S WORLD

We understand that this world is broken, sinful, and fallen, and many dark and evil qualities can be seen, felt, and experienced here. But beauty still exists. There is so much in this world that is true, honorable, just, pure, lovely, commendable, excellent, and worthy of praise. These qualities that Paul mentions here were commended by pagans, not just believers. There is much in this world that is worthy of our focus and commendation. Paul said, *"Think about those things. Think about the beautiful things in this world."*

## THE BEAUTY IN THE WORD OF GOD

Another source of beauty exists for us. We can think about the beautiful things that are in the Word of God. The Word of God is *true*. The Word of God is *honorable*. The Word of God is *just*. The Word of God is *pure*. The Word of God is *lovely*. The Word of God is *commendable*. The Word of God is *excellent*. The Word of God is *worthy of praise*. We find these qualities *in* the Word, so we must fill our minds *with* the Word of God.

## THE BEAUTY IN GOD'S WONDERFUL SON

We see beauty in God's world, we see beauty in God's Word, but we also see beauty in God's wonderful Son, Jesus. What we have been given in Philippians 4:8 is a portrait of Jesus! When we focus on Jesus, what do we discover about him? We are continually delighted to see that Jesus is *true*, Jesus is *honorable*, Jesus is *just*, Jesus is *pure*, Jesus is *lovely*, Jesus is *commendable*, Jesus is *excellent*, and Jesus is so, so very *worthy of praise*.

We protect our treasure of peace by focusing our thinking on beauty—the things that are beautiful in God's world, in God's Word, and in God's wonderful Son, Jesus. We guard our minds by actively thinking about these gifts from our Heavenly Father.

Finally, there is one final aspect of Paul's prescribed regimen for peace. Along with maintaining the right *attitude* and the right *attention*, we must also take the right *action.* Paul challenged those first-century believers, and he challenges us today with the same admonition:

> *What you have learned and received and heard and*
> *seen in me—practice these things, and the*
> *God of peace will be with you.*
> (Philippians 4:9)

If we desire to be people who overcome the paralysis of fear, then we must be people of action. And the right action is to put into practice those things that we have *learned* and have *received*. Learning and receiving must always travel together on the journey of spiritual growth. The word "learned" is connected to the same term that is translated as *disciple*. Paul is calling the Philippians to remember the things he shared with them during their discipleship. The word "received" has to do with the *body of truth* they received—the teachings of Jesus and the applications of the gospel's message.

Then, in a very personal manner, Paul reminds them of what they had heard from him personally in those precious days they shared together. He reminds them of all the moments he invested his life into theirs. They did not just *hear* him teach; they *saw* him walk out those teachings. Paul had communicated more than just a message to them; he also modeled a way of life. He challenged these believers not only to remember his words but also to follow his ways. Humbly, he could honestly say to them, "The things that you learned from me as I discipled you, the things that I communicated to you, the Word of the Gospel, the message of Christ, the things that you have heard and seen in my manner of living—*you do these things*, and the God of peace will be with you."

> Peace is the manifested presence of
> the God of peace.

## MODELS OF PEACE

If we are going to experience peace, then we need to follow role models of peace. Who are your role models? Some of us have no peace because the people we model our lives after are not peace-filled. Paul was a peace-filled man. He was filled with the Spirit of God, the Word of God, and the love of God. In an environment of almost constant opposition and persecution, Paul remained a man characterized by peace. Even from prison, he could joyfully and confidently say, "Now, you follow me as I follow Christ, and you will know peace."

This call from Paul is much more than a command; it is an invitation to experience God. He promised, "The God of peace will be with you." One of the results of a wasted life is the absence of peace. "The way of peace they have not known" (Isa. 59:8) is the tragic commentary on the self-directed life of those who do not follow the Lord. Peace is not something we achieve; it is a gift of God himself. Peace is the manifested presence of the God of peace. To live without peace is to live without God. Without a doubt, that is the greatest of all robberies! Sadly, it is a robbery in which people victimize themselves because the Lord offers himself and his peace to all as a free gift.

God offers this ultimate and complete peace to you today, my friend. The gift of his peace can be yours. "Therefore, since we have been justified by faith, we have peace with God through our Lord Jesus Christ" (Rom. 5:1-3). Peace *with* God was made by Jesus, and the peace *of* God will be guarded in your life *by* Jesus. "And the peace of God, which surpasses all understanding, will guard your hearts and minds in Christ Jesus" (Phil. 4:7). The Prince of Peace is calling today: "Peace I leave with you; my peace I give to you. Not as the world gives do I give to you. Let not your hearts be troubled, neither let them be afraid" (John 14:27).

## PRAYER

*Almighty Lord, thank you for being the God of peace and for making peace with us, rebellious sinners, through the sacrifice of your precious Son. Thank you, that being justified through faith we have peace with God through our Lord Jesus Christ. May the Prince of Peace rule and reign as Captain of our souls. Help us to stand guard over this gift of peace that you have so graciously given us. May we not allow the toxin of fear to contaminate our minds, robbing us of that peace that Jesus won through his great victory. Because of his victory, help us to choose joy today. May we rejoice in the Lord, who is forever worthy of our praise. In his mighty and victorious name, we pray.*

*Amen.*

# R.E.A.P. GUIDE

**R**EAD
- Read Philippians 4:8-9.
- What lessons do you see the Holy Spirit teaching you in this text?

**E**XAMINE
- Apostle Paul has been speaking in Philippians 4:8-9 about one main spiritual reality God wants each of his people to have. What is that reality according to verse 9?
- How would you summarize the responsibility Paul says believers have, in verses 8-9, to live in this spiritual reality?

**A**PPLY
- What should we be thinking about and filling our minds with, in keeping with Paul's commands in verses 8-9?
- These qualities Paul lists are most evident in the life of Jesus Christ. What can you recall about the Lord that helps you better meditate on these qualities?

**P**RAY
- Using the "PRAY" acronym, respond with **P**raise to the Lord, **R**epent of sins this Bible passage has revealed to you, **A**sk the Lord for any requests you have, and **Y**ield to his will.

# - 8 -

# SHELTERED IN GOD

*He who dwells in the shelter of the Most High*
*will abide in the shadow of the Almighty.*
*I will say to the Lord, "My refuge and my fortress,*
*my God, in whom I trust."*
*For he will deliver you from the snare of the fowler*
*and from the deadly pestilence.*
*He will cover you with his pinions,*
*and under his wings you will find refuge;*
*his faithfulness is a shield and buckler.*
***You will not fear*** *the terror of the night,*
*nor the arrow that flies by day,*
*nor the pestilence that stalks in darkness,*
*nor the destruction that wastes at noonday.*
*A thousand may fall at your side,*
*ten thousand at your right hand,*
*but it will not come near you.*
*You will only look with your eyes*
*and see the recompense of the wicked.*

*Because you have made the Lord your dwelling*
*place—the Most High, who is my refuge—*
*no evil shall be allowed to befall you,*
*no plague come near your tent.*
*For he will command his angels concerning you*
*to guard you in all your ways.*
*On their hands they will bear you up,*
*lest you strike your foot against a stone.*
*You will tread on the lion and the adder;*
*the young lion and the serpent you will*
*trample underfoot.*
*"Because he holds fast to me in love, I will deliver*
*him; I will protect him, because he knows my*
*name.*
*When he calls to me, I will answer him;*
*I will be with him in trouble;*
*I will rescue him and honor him.*
*With long life I will satisfy him*
*and show him my salvation."*
(Psalm 91:1-16)

B illionaire David Geffen has been involved in the
production of several noteworthy films for many years as
part of "DreamWorks SKG." (SKG stands for Steven Spielberg,
Jeffrey Katzenberg, and David Geffen.) On March 28, 2020, in
the middle of the coronavirus epidemic, Mr. Geffen produced a
picture that, without doubt, was publicly shown for the briefest
time of any of his other projects—for one day. Actually, it was
not a film but a photograph of his 550 million dollar luxury
superyacht anchored in the Caribbean near the Grenadine
Island chain.

Mr. Geffen posted on Instagram a photo of a sunset with
its fading golden beams of light shimmering behind his
beautiful 550-million-dollar vessel. Geffen's post on Instagram
read, "Sunset, last night...isolated in the Grenadines avoiding

the virus..." You could almost hear the huge public groan in response, saying, *"Really? That's the message you're sending out? Isolating from the virus on your 550-million-dollar yacht at sunset in the Grenadine Islands of the Caribbean?!"* As I said, the post did not stay up very long.

Most of us recall experiencing a little different kind of "sheltering" during that time period. Regardless, whether sheltered on a 550-million-dollar yacht or sheltered at home, however humbling that might be, there exists a virus that can creep into and infect any residence, and that is the plague of fear. This epidemic of fear is ancient, universal, and truly deadly. But, thank God, a cure exists that is completely effective and completely free.

Let us turn to someone who knew what it meant to be deeply infected by the virus of fear but also experienced a vaccination that turned his worry into worship. On many occasions, our friend David struggled deeply with fear, but he also experienced the sufficiency of God, which filled his heart with joy and confidence, so much so that he had to write a song of praise about it. The song that David wrote regarding the victory over fear was inspired by God and included in our Bibles as Psalm 91—one of the most beloved Psalms of David.

## PSALM 91

The key to this passage is found in verse 5 when David says,

> ***You will not fear*** *the terror of the night,*
> *nor the arrow that flies by day...*

This Psalm is amazing in so many ways. We could not begin to cover the depth of it in an entire book, let alone one chapter. Psalm 91 is filled with meditations from the shepherd-king, David, to nourish the souls of God's sheep throughout their journey home. It is a song of shelter. In fact, it is a song of "shelter" in safety from fear. What makes this song so unusual and so beautiful is that God himself is celebrated as the believer's ultimate shelter.

### THE PERSONAL RESIDENCE FOR GOD'S PEOPLE
(Psalm 91:1-2)

In verses 1-2, notice how David describes the personal place of residence and shelter for the people of God.

> *He who dwells in the shelter of the Most High will*
> *abide in the shadow of the Almighty. I will say to the*
> *Lord, "My refuge and my fortress,*
> *my God, in whom I trust."*
> (Psalm 91:1-2)

The setting for this song is in the Judaean wilderness, which is truly a wilderness, a region that receives very little rainfall and is almost devoid of any vegetation. It is incredibly hot during the day and frigid at night. This is the place David had to consider his home for lengthy periods of time, especially when he was fleeing for his life from King Saul. Again, no vegetation, very little water, and burning heat, but David finds shelter in this Judaean wilderness. In the deep canyons formed by the steep barren cliffs, David and his men found that the shadows provided them wonderful shelter from the elements and the relentless spies of King Saul.

Anyone who has ever been in a very arid climate and felt the burning rays of the sun knows the immediate relief experienced when stepping into any available shade. David and his men experienced that relief. They also found safety in the shadows formed by the barren rocks because the brightness of the sunlight and the barrenness of the landscape afforded no cover from their many enemies. Going into those canyons formed by the steep cliffs, David found not just shadows but a home in which he came to consider his refuge and his fortress.

The cooling shadows brought David *physical* and emotional rest for his soul. But there, in the wilderness, he also found spiritual rest. While hiding in those canyons and shadows, David recognized that they were only a physical expression of his ultimate place of safety, shelter, and refuge, which was God himself.

That is the reason David writes this beautiful Psalm. By God's grace, he begins to see his circumstances and surroundings in a very different light. They remind him of his supreme place of safety and shelter—the Lord his God.

### David's place of hiding
### became a place of worship.

In verse 2, David gives voice to his choice of praise, "I will say to the Lord, 'My refuge and my fortress, my God, in whom I trust.'" We are permitted to listen to the working of David's thoughts of worship, "God, it is not these canyons that are my shelter. *You are my shelter.* You are my dwelling place. You are the place of safety for me. You are, for me, an unimaginable residence." Yes, David is living in a safe place, in the safety of his God.

Dear friend, I want you to know that God is still that place of shelter. The God we worship, the God of David, is shelter indeed. He is still the refuge. He is still the fortress. And he is still the same God. But who are the people who can experience God's shelter as David did 3,000 years ago? There is a very clear answer to that question. Those who can experience God's refuge are those who **trust**.

It is essential to unite that concept of "trust" in verse 2 with what David has just shared in the opening line of his song. "He who **dwells** in the shelter of the Most High..." In your Bible, circle the word "dwell" and connect it to the word in verse two—"trust." Who is the one who dwells in the shadow of the Almighty? Who is the one who can say, "God is my refuge?" It is the person who **trusts** in the Lord and who has an unqualified reliance on God. People who trust God experience God as their place of shelter. It is the reality of God that is only experienced by *faith*. Faith is the substance of our souls that connects us with the ultimate reality of our living God. And this is exactly where David takes us in his song, into the reality of God himself.

### THE POWERFUL REALITIES FOR GOD'S PEOPLE
(Psalm 91:3-13)

Notice in verses 3 through 13 that as David is sharing about the beautiful and powerful realities available for God's people, he is sharing about his "dwelling place," his "shelter," his "refuge," and his "fortress." These are all descriptions of his personal residence, where he lives, sheltered in the Almighty—God, his refuge; God, his dwelling place. But, even as David goes out into the activities and inevitable challenges of life, God is still his reality. And so, beginning in verse 3 through verse 13, David promises that the daily reality of God he has personally experienced is available to God's people, regardless of what any day may bring. The daily reality of God is for all who trust in him. God is *that* real. God is not wishful thinking; God *is* reality.

The word David uses eight times to express the promise of God's living reality is the word *will*. David says in verse 3, "He *will* deliver you." In verse 4, "He *will* cover you." In verse 5, "You *will* not fear." In verse 7, "It *will* not come near you." In verse 8, "You *will* only look with your eyes and see the recompense of the wicked." Verse 11, "He *will* command his angels to watch over you." In verse 12, "They *will* bear you up." Then, in verse 13, "You *will* tread on the lion and on the adder..." These are promises of God's reality. These verses truly share the *will* of God.

Then, notice *two amazing images* of how real God is to David. I hope these images rest on your heart as you continue to meditate on Psalm 91. Notice the images God inspires David to use regarding the reality of God to his people. First, God uses the image of a *mother bird,* and then he uses the image of a *military battle.* The image of a mother bird is one of the most beautiful passages in all of the Psalms of David:

> *For he will deliver you from the snare of the fowler*
> *and from the deadly pestilence.*
> *He will cover you with his pinions,*
> *and under his wings you will find refuge;*
> *his faithfulness is a shield and buckler.*
> (Psalm 91:3-4)

What a sweet, tender, and yet startling image. It is an image that no one would dare use for Almighty God unless God himself inspired David to use it. It is the image of God Almighty covering his people like a *mother bird* would cover her chicks. This is the image of the Lord God spreading himself out over his people...an image of absolute love. It conveys a love so great that it is willing to sacrifice, even to the point of death.

My friend, that is precisely what God did. He loved that much. God *so loved* the world through the outstretched arms of his Son, Jesus Christ. Jesus used this image of the mother bird, evoked by David, as he was riding into Jerusalem on the day we now call Palm Sunday. People were shouting, "Hosanna to the Son of David; blessed is the he who comes in the name of the Lord; hosanna in the highest" (Matt. 21:9). The Bible says that Jesus, in the midst of that praise, was weeping and crying out,

> *"O Jerusalem, Jerusalem, the city that kills the*
> *prophets and stones those who are sent to it! How*
> *often would I have gathered your children together as*
> *a hen gathers her brood under her wings,*
> *and you were not willing!"*
> (Luke 13:34)

Five days later, Jesus did spread himself out over his people. The Bible tells us that though Jesus was rejected as the rightful King, yet he went to the cross wearing a crown. Yes, the crowned One on the cross, with his arms outstretched in love, covered his people with the sacrifice of his own body and his blood. He spread himself in substitution and sacrifice and absorbed the wrath due to sinners—giving his life that we might live. This is the God we serve. A God that is so loving, tender, and kind that he came to this earth and spread himself out, taking upon himself the judgment *our sins deserved*. What a God we serve! How precious he is! That God is our same God today, and he cares for us with a love beyond imagination. Under his wings, there is no fear.

> Under God's wings,
> there is no fear.

In this shelter of the Almighty, the shadow beneath the cross-centered love of God, there is absolutely no fear.

Now, notice one other image that David uses in this beautiful song—the image of a military conflict or battle. This God who loves us with such tenderness will also be with us in the midst of battle! David says in verse 4 that the Lord will be "a shield and buckler." Then, in verses 5 and 6, he promises,

> *You will not fear the terror of the night,*
> *nor the arrow that flies by day,*
> *nor the pestilence that stalks in darkness,*
> *nor the destruction that wastes at noonday.*

David continues with the imagery of warfare in verse 7:

> *A thousand may fall at your side,*
> *ten thousand at your right hand,*

*but it will not come near you.*
(Psalm 91:7)

Again, these are graphic images of battle, but in the midst of the battle, God's chosen ones are secure. And then, as if these promises were not enough in describing God's protection of his people, David declares that heavenly angels are assigned to us to help us during our time of struggle here on earth:

> *For he will command his angels concerning you*
> *to guard you in all your ways.*
> *On their hands they will bear you up,*
> *lest you strike your foot against a stone.*
> (Psalm 91:11-12)

Hebrews 1:14 speaks in the same way regarding these angels who are our unseen guardians:

> *Are they not all ministering spirits sent out to serve*
> *for the sake of those who are to inherit salvation?*
> (Hebrews 1:14)

The angels are "ministering spirits" sent forth to serve us, those who will be the heirs of salvation. When we are in times of deepest trials, we are not alone. The Holy Spirit is with us, along with angels assigned for our care to provide for and protect us. We are often in the midst of spiritual and physical struggles and conflict, but indwelt by the Spirit of God, we are upheld by the angels of God. No wonder David can assure us, "You will not fear!" (Ps. 91:5).

Regarding this passage in Psalm 91, I recall something Tim Keller, the pastor of Redeemer Presbyterian Church in New York City, said during a session at a ministry conference. He specifically referred to verses 11 and 12 in his address entitled "Satanic Exposition." What a title! He called it "Satanic Exposition" because this is the very passage Satan quoted as he tempted the Lord Jesus Christ to cast himself down from the pinnacle of the temple if he were the Son of God.

Yes, Satan uses Scripture! What was Satan trying to do? He was trying to keep Jesus from fulfilling the will of God. He was trying to tempt Jesus into trusting *in his own way* rather than committing himself entirely to *the will of God*. In effect, Satan was saying, *"You don't have to suffer, Jesus. There is another way that you can still do the will of God without suffering."* Satan knows how to take Scripture out of context and twist it.

The Lord Jesus Christ trusted God completely. He knew that his Father's will was the way of salvation, and he committed himself even to the point of unimaginable suffering. It is passages like these and others that are also twisted in the name of so-called "Christianity," saying that if we have enough faith, then we don't have to suffer. We are told that we can create our own reality, and when we speak the words of faith, it will be done. I trust you know this is completely contrary to the Word of God and such blasphemous teaching. The Lord Jesus himself was called to suffer in order to accomplish God's purpose of salvation, and the Bible says that we are also called to *follow in his steps*. We are called to suffer at times. In fact, we often suffer not because we are *out* of the will of God, but in truth, we will suffer because we are *in* the will of God.

God has ordained that in our suffering and trial, we will know him as our dwelling place, our shelter, our refuge, our strength, and our fortress. That, my friend, is *Spirit-directed exposition* that the Lord wants us to apply to our hearts.

Finally, notice the promises the Lord makes in this song of David in the closing phrases of God's praise. David sings about the *promised rewards* for the Lord's people. Yes, there is the reality of suffering and struggle, but God will reward us. Even though it will be difficult, the difficulties will seem like nothing compared to the overwhelming privileges which our God will make known to us.

## *ALREADY, BUT NOT YET*

We live in what the teachers of the Reformation often designated as the *"already-not yet"* season of our salvation. We are already delivered, but not yet completely delivered. We are already healed but not yet completely healed. We are already children of Heaven, but we are not yet in Heaven. We are already God's glorified ones, but we are not yet glorified in his presence. This is our existence as we make our journey home—*already, but not yet.*

## *THE PROMISED REWARDS FOR GOD'S PEOPLE*
(Ps. 91:14-16)

My friend, the promises of God are absolutely certain. There is the present reality of God and his love for us. There is the present reality of his protection, but he has promised rewards for his people. God speaks through David regarding these promises in verses 14 through 16:

> *"Because **he holds fast to me** in love, I will deliver him;*
> *I will protect him, because he knows my name.*
> *When he calls to me, I will answer him;*
> *I will be with him in trouble;*
> *I will rescue him and honor him.*
> *With long life I will satisfy him*
> *and show him my salvation."*

In these verses, the Lord promises three great rewards for those who have him as their dwelling place and for those who find shelter in him as their home. First of all, God promises that he will hold us.

## God will "hold" us.

First of all, God promises that he will hold us. Verse 14 states, "Because he holds fast to me in love, I will deliver him; I will protect him because he knows my name." You see, when we are holding fast to the Lord, *he is holding fast to us*. Our response in taking hold of him is because he has taken hold of us. We hold him, and he holds us. That is the union that we have in Christ. And the Lord promises we will be held by him. He will hold us fast. We will not be lost. We will not be allowed to drift away. We are held by him because we have come to know his name. What does that mean to *"know his name*?" It means we know him for who he really is by living experience. We do not just know *about* him; we *know him*. We are held to him by a loving union that is eternal life itself.

## God will "hear" us.

The second reward that God promises to those who reside by faith in him is that *he will hear us*.

> *"When he calls to me, I will answer him;*
> *I will be with him in trouble;*
> *I will rescue him and honor him."*
> (Psalm 91:15)

Notice, "when he calls...I will answer." That is a promise from God that in times of trouble, he is "a very present help in time of need" (Ps. 46:1). The Lord is not distant, "The Lord is at hand," as Paul shares in Philippians 4:5. When we call, he is listening because we are his children and he cares for us so tenderly. When we call, he listens. One of the great and priceless rewards for the people of God is that our God is also our Heavenly Father, whose ear is always attentive to the voices of his dear children. When we call upon the Lord in times of trouble, we can be rest assured that he will hear us.

## God will "honor" us.

The final reward the Lord promises us in this beautiful song is that as we make him our refuge and fortress, he will graciously honor us. How amazing is our Lord, who gives us himself as our home and also gives us honor!

> *"With long life I will satisfy him*
> *and show him my salvation."*
> (Psalm 91:16)

Now, someone might say, *"How can it be that the Lord gives long life to people who trust in him, believe in him, and hold to him as their dwelling place when so many Christians don't live a long life? They are taken from us early in life?"* What is the answer to that? The answer is this: the length of a person's life is not measured in the quantity of days but in the *quality* of days. For Christians, there is no limit to their days because to be absent from the body is to be present with the Lord (2 Cor. 5:8). The Bible says that we have eternal life, and one day we will go to be with the Lord and it will be an everlasting day, a day without end, worshiping in his presence.

We *do* have a *quantity* of days! But on Earth, what matters most is that there is a quality of life in the number of days the Lord gives us. The Lord promised abundant life. Jesus said, "I came that they may have life and have it abundantly" (John 10:10). That is his promise of quantity and quality of days, life forever, and the promise of life right now. Being a Christian does not just mean there is life after death. To be a Christian means there is life *before and after death.* We have real life now, and we will have incredible everlasting life in the presence of the Lord one day, a day that will last forever.

Have you ever asked yourself, "What is life? Is it just a succession of days?" In the Bible, Jesus tells us what life really is. When praying in the Garden of Gethsemane, Jesus said this to his Father:

*And this is eternal life, **that they know you, the only true God, and Jesus Christ whom you have sent.** I glorified you on earth, having accomplished the work that you gave me to do.*
(John 17:3-4)

Jesus defined eternal life in these words of prayer to his Heavenly Father, "...that they know you, the only true God, and Jesus Christ whom you have sent." Eternal life, then, is knowing God personally through his Son, Jesus Christ. Through faith in Jesus, we experience eternal life and also *true* life.

The Lord's promise to those who trust in him is that *he will show them his salvation.* His salvation is Jesus. The name Jesus means "Jehovah is salvation." It is in Jesus Christ that we truly come to know God and to know everlasting life in his love. It is in the Lord Jesus Christ that we find our true shelter, comfort, and safety. In him, and through him, and because of him, we have this abiding promise:

### Fear not!

## *PRAYER*

*Heavenly Father, we thank you and praise you for being our dwelling place for all generations. You are our refuge and our fortress forever and ever. Thank you, Lord, that in our wilderness experiences, during our trials and challenges, you are our abiding place and our everlasting joy. In you, there is life and life to the fullest. And we thank you, Lord, that we have a place of safety where fear cannot reign because Jesus reigns. We praise you, that where Christ reigns, peace reigns. May your peace reign in our hearts. We give you praise for this victory that overcomes the world, the victory of our faith in the One who is victorious —the Lord Jesus Christ, in whose name we pray.*

*Amen.*

# R.E.A.P. GUIDE

**R**EAD
- Read Psalm 91.
- What lessons do you see the Holy Spirit teaching you in this text?

**E**XAMINE
- The main idea of this Psalm appears in verses 1-2. How would you express the main idea in your own words?
- What is revealed about God in verses 1-2, 4, and 9?
- Verses 3-10 describe the special protection of God's people. In what types of situations does God protect his people?
- Verses 8b and 10b describe a specific context for God's protection. What is that context?
- What is God's part in providing this protection (11-16)?
- What is the believer's part in receiving this protection (14-16)?

**A**PPLY
- In what ways may we apply this Psalm to our situation of physical or emotional stress?
- What are some ways this Psalm could be misapplied to times of personal trials?
- What is revealed about our God that is always applicable?

**P**RAY
- Using the "PRAY" acronym, respond with **P**raise to the Lord, **R**epent of sins this Bible passage has revealed to you, **A**sk the Lord for any requests you have, and **Y**ield to his will.

God does not want His children to simply *believe* in Him. He wants them to *experience* Him and know the sweetness of His loving provision.

**SonLight** is an inspirational tool for Christians to truly *experience* God on a daily basis.

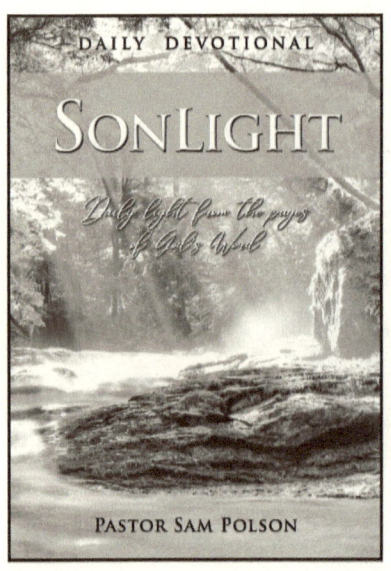

Pastor Sam Polson leads you through the *New Testament, Psalms, and Proverbs,* all the while encouraging you with special antidotes and insightful wisdom, in a way that only a *seasoned pastor* can!

**ISBN: 978-1-643700-30-4**

In **Pathways,** inspirational author and pastor
Sam Polson shares words of wisdom for hope-filled living
*365 days a year!*

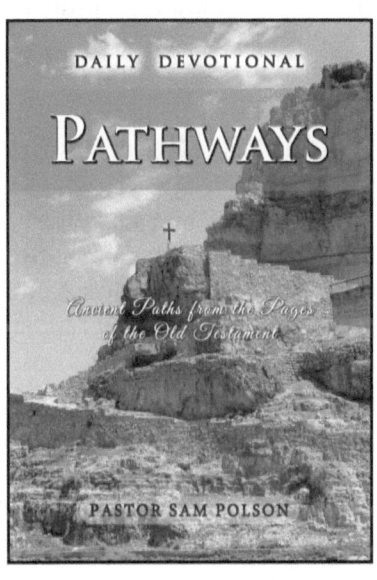

In today's *ever-growing, complex world,*
you can abide evermore in God's love and grace,
*preparing your hearts and minds for what lies
ahead* with Pastor Polson's new
daily devotional *Pathways.*

**ISBN: 978-1-956218-23-7**

# ABOUT
# CLIMBING ANGEL PUBLISHING

Climbing Angel Publishing shares stories of hope and encouragement, aids in the gathering together of community, and supports the process of betterment. The following books are available at your leading online bookstores.

## ADULT BOOKS: (Romans 8:28-30)

*In His Image* by Sam Polson
(English, Romanian, Mandarin & Spanish)
*By Faith* by Sam Polson (English & Romanian)
*My Birthday Gift to Jesus* by Lisa Soland
*Without Ceasing* by Dr. Dennis Davidson
*SonLight: Daily Light from the Pages of God's Word*
by Sam Polson
*Corona Victus: Conquering the Virus of Fear*
by Sam Polson (English & Romanian)
*Art Bushing: His Diary, Letters, & Photographs of WWII*
by Art Bushing
*Art & Dotty: His Diary, Their Letters & Photographs of WWII*
by Art Bushing
*Trimisul* by Stan Johnson (Romanian)
*Life Changing Prayer* by Sam Polson
*The Climbing Angel Christmas Treasury*,
an anthology by a variety of authors
*J. Calvin Coolidge: Letters from the Korean War*
by J. Calvin Coolidge
*Stories from Kingman, AZ: The Heart of Historic Route 66*
by Loren B. Wilson
*Pathways: Ancient Paths from the Pages of the Old Testament*
by Sam Polson
*Fear Not* by Sam Polson

# THE SINGLE SERMON SERIES: (1 Pet. 3:15)

*Jesus is Alive!* by Mike Sager
*My Mother's Bible* by Sam Polson
*The Lost Boys* by Jake Bishop
*Melchizedek: A Shadow of Christ* by Jerry Scheumann
*A Servant of Christ* by James Alan Lynch
*Dreaming God's Dream* by Dr. Al Cage
*Resisting Sin* by Colin Hughes
*A Call to Christians* by Chris Reed

# CHILDREN'S BOOKS: (Philippians 4:8)

*The Christmas Tree Angel* by Lisa Soland
*The Unmade Moose* by Lisa Soland
*Thump* by Lisa Soland
*Somebunny To Love* by Lisa Soland
(English & Mandarin)
*The Truth About God's Rainbow* by Lisa Soland
*God's Promises* by Lisa Soland
*The Boy & The Bagel Necklace* by Lisa Soland
*God's Hands and Feet* by Lisa Soland
*I Like To Be Quiet* by Joni Caldwell
*Wheels Off!* by Karlie Saumier
*Ella's Trip of a Lifetime* by Melanie Ewbank
*Because You Are Mine* by Gayle Childress Greene
*Jeremy Plays the Blues* by Amy Oden Simpson
*Bad Hair Day* by Jasmyne Simpkins
*I Like To Read* by Joni Caldwell
*Trunks Up!* by Karlie Saumier
*Perusha's Paradise* by Bette Reed Smith
*Ruby and the Treasure Within* by Tonya Celeste Hobbs
*Abby, the Wonder Dog & her Warrior Princess*
by Melanie Ewbank
*The Christmas Coat* by Lisa Soland
*Danger Around the Bend* by Karlie Saumier